THE RISE AND FALL
OF THE
ROMAN REPUBLIC

LESSONS FOR MODERN AMERICA

by Steve Bonta, PhD

The John Birch Society
Appleton, Wisconsin

First Printing . . . . May 2006

Published by
The John Birch Society
Post Office Box 8040
Appleton, Wisconsin 54912
920-749-3780

JBS.*org*

Printed in the United States of America
LC Control Number
2006926981
ISBN: 1-881919-11-0

The chapters in this book are adapted from a series of articles on the rise and fall of the Roman Republic originally appearing in *The New American* magazine during 2004–05.

CONTENTS

Maps & Illustrations vi

Introduction vii

Chronology viii

1. The Birth of the Republic 1

2. The Republic Matures 13

3. The Imperial Republic 23

4. Rise of the Welfare-Warfare State 39

5. Civil War and Despotism 47

6. Cicero, Catiline, and Conspiracy 57

7. The Rise of Caesarism 69

8. From Republic to Empire 85

9. Rome's Dark Night of Tyranny 97

10. Lessons of Rome 111

    For Further Reading 121

    Index 125

    About the Author 137

Maps & Illustrations

The Vestal Virgins. 1
Rome Triumphant. 5
Numa Pompilius 7
Roman Soldiers. 8-9
The Sacking of Rome by the Gauls 11
The Roman Forum 13
Appius Claudius and the other Decemvirs 16
Virginius Saves Virginia's Honor. 18
Scipio Africanus. 21
Hannibal Crossing the Alps 24
Rome and Carthage (map) 31
Rome destroys Carthage, 146 B.C. 35
Caius Gracchus flees mob. 39
The Gracchi Brothers 40
Caius Marius. 45
The Defeat of Spartacus 47
Roman Republic circa 85 B.C. (map) 51
Sulla's Fateful March 52
Cicero Denounces Catiline in the Roman Senate 57
Catilinarian Conspiracy Unmasked 59
Gallic Warriors 61
Pompey the Great. 62
Julius Caesar. 67
A Triumphant Julius Caesar 69
Gauls Submit to Caesar 73
Pompey Flees Rome. 76
Caesar Refuses Crown. 79
Caesar's Assassination 83
The Death of Cicero. 85
Caesar's Funeral 87
Roman Empire at its Greatest Extent (map) 89
Battle of Actium. 92
Cleopatra on Her Ship. 94
Alaric the Goth 97
First Century Emperors 101
Nero Martyrs Christians. 105
The Vandals Sack Rome 107
The Roman Forum 111
Roman Military Purges 115
U.S. Supreme Court Building and Roman Parthenon 117

Introduction

By all accounts, Rome in the eighth century B.C. was little more than an armed camp of brigands. Yet within seven hundred years, this squalid, warlike settlement became the greatest man-made power the world had ever seen, mistress of most of Europe, North Africa, Asia Minor and the Middle East. Ancient Rome was the incubator for Christianity, the repository of Western civilization for over a thousand years, and the setting for much of the greatest historical drama — and many of the most extraordinary characters — ever to occupy the human stage.

Rome rose to unexampled heights, only to fall with a shock that still reverberates across the centuries. Unlike the great civilizations that preceded her — Egypt, Elam, Sumer, Babylon, Carthage, and others — Rome's legacy was far more than jumbled ruins. Of Rome has been preserved a vast literature, a code of laws, and many of our political, cultural, artistic and religious forms. For instead of collapsing utterly, like its predecessors, Rome broke into fragments which were transformed into the political and religious institutions that served as a foundation for modern Western civilization.

America's Founding Fathers, as well as their European contemporaries, were fascinated with Rome, because the Western world in the 18th century had only recently attained the wealth, power, and vitality of Roman civilization at its peak. The marvels of Roman engineering, architecture, law, art, and literature were mimicked in Europe and America for centuries, until the industrial age finally allowed Europe and America to outstrip and eclipse the achievements of ancient Rome.

But the mystique of Rome persists. The lessons of the rise and fall of Rome resonate in our age, when a single power consumed by imperial ambition and threatened by moral decline — the United States of America — seems to be slouching down the same path to oblivion that the Romans once followed.

Chronology

753 B.C. Founding of Rome

509 B.C. Founding of the Republic

290 B.C. Pyrrhus invade Italy

264 B.C. Outbreak of First Punic War

241 B.C. End of First Punic War

218 B.C. Outbreak of Second Punic War

216 B.C. Battle of Cannae

202 B.C. End of Second Punic War

186 B.C. Suppression of the Bacchic Cult

167 B.C. Final Triumph of Rome over Macedonian Greeks

149 B.C. Outbreak of Third Pubic War

146 B.C. Destruction of Carthage

200 B.C. The Imperial Republic

132 B.C. Death of Tiberius Gracchus

121 B.C. Death of Caius Gracchus

112 B.C. Outbreak of Jugurthine War

105 B.C. End of Jugurthine War

Battle of Arausin

Rise of the Welfare-Warfare State

102 B.C. Battle of Aquae Sextiae

101 B.C. Battle of Vercellae

91 B.C. Outbreak of the Social War

88 B.C. Outbreak of the First Mithridatic War

87-86 B.C. Marian Purges

84 B.C. Sulla returns from the East

82 B.C. Sulla defeats Marian forces

78 B.C. Death of Sulla

63 B.C. Exposure of the Catilinarian Conspiracy

62 B.C. Defeat and death of Catiline

59 B.C. Julius Caesar elected consul and First Triumvirate formed

58 B.C. Caesar's Gallic campaigns begin

55 B.C. Caesar invades Britain for first time

53 B.C. Crassus' defeat and death at Carrhae

49 B.C. Caesar' forces invade Italy

48 B.C. Defeat of Pompey at Pharsalus

44 B.C. Assassination of Julius Caesar

42-31 B.C. From Republic to Empire

42 B.C. Battle of Philippi

14 A.D. Death of Caesar Augustus

14-37 A.D. Reign of Tiberius

37-41 A.D. Reign of Caligula

54-68 A.D. Reign of Nero

64 A.D. Great Fire destroys Rome

70 A.D. Destruction of Jerusalem

180 A.D. Death of Marcus Aurelius

192 A.D. Commodus strangled by gladiator

306-307 A.D. Reign of Constantine the Great

378 A.D. Battle of Hadrianople

410 A.D. Alaric the Goth sacks Rome

455 A.D. Genseric the Vandal sacks Rome

CHAPTER 1

THE BIRTH OF THE REPUBLIC

Rome's astonishing ascent was due primarily to the moral sensibilities of her people and the limitation of government power.

As with most ancient nations, the origins of Rome are clouded by legend. The first inhabitants of what became the city-state of Rome may have been refugees from defeated Troy, led by the semi-legendary hero Aeneas. Rome's greatest poet, Virgil, said as much in his immortal epic, *The Aeneid*. And many historians who lived in ancient Rome, whose works have been handed down to our day — men like Appian and Livy — claimed the same.

According to Livy, Aeneas, along with a number of exiled Trojans, arrived on the Adriatic coast of Italy, where he received

The Vestal Virgins were the guardians of the sacred fire at the temple of the goddess Vesta that came to symbolize the Roman state. Violation of their oath of virginity was punished by being buried alive.

permission to settle there from Latinus, a local chieftain. Livy said of the meeting:

> [Latinus,] struck with admiration both at the noble charac-
> ter of the nation and the hero [Aeneas], and at their spirit,
> ready alike for peace or war ... ratified the pledge of future
> friendship by clasping hands. Thereupon a treaty was con-
> cluded between the chiefs, and mutual greetings passed
> between the armies: Aeneas was hospitably entertained
> at the house of Latinus; there Latinus, in the presence of
> his household gods, cemented the public league by a fam-
> ily one, by giving Aeneas his daughter in marriage. This
> event fully confirmed the Trojans in the hope of at length
> terminating their wanderings by a lasting and permanent
> settlement.

Thereafter, the two races intermarried and called themselves Latins. They eventually established a settlement at Alba Longa, where the twin brothers Romulus and Remus, the supposed founders of the city of Rome, were born. Romulus and Remus had been abandoned as children after the illegitimate and ty-rannical king of Alba Longa, Amulius, tried to have them killed. As adults, Romulus and Remus deposed Amulius and restored his brother Numitor as the legitimate king to the throne of Alba Longa. For their pains, Romulus and Remus received permis-sion to found a new city on the Tiber.

Of the time between the traditional founding of Rome around 753 B.C. with the monarchy of Romulus, and the birth of the Roman Republic in about 509 B.C. with the expulsion of the Tarquins, a dynasty of Etruscan kings, we know nothing not colored by legend. Yet there is no reason not to believe that Romulus existed, and that he was, as Plutarch and Livy both assert, the first Roman king. Whether legendary or real, Romu-lus is depicted as a violent, warlike individual, the most ruth-less member of a very rough crowd. He reputedly murdered his brother Remus, and went to war with the Sabines because his men had raped the Sabine women. Whether true or not, these stories are certainly in keeping with the warlike spirit the Romans cultivated from the very foundation of their city.

State of War

With only a few brief interludes, Rome was perpetually at war from the time of the Tarquins to the ascent of Caesar Augustus. As Alexander Hamilton observed, Rome was "never sated of carnage and conquest." Like Sparta, Rome, both as a monarchy and as a republic, was organized along military lines. Every able-bodied Roman male was eligible for the annual draft into military service, and many served in Rome's army throughout their prime years. It was not until the time of Marius in the late second century B.C. that Rome professionalized her military. So pervasive was the military in Roman political culture that even the senators were known as "conscript fathers." Much of Rome's success can be attributed to her fanatical attention to military order and to the cultivation of virtues conducive to military strength: unswerving loyalty, obedience, frugality, and disregard for peril to life and limb.

From her remotest beginnings, Rome enjoyed an almost uninterrupted string of military successes, at first over hostile neighboring tribes like the Aequans, the Volscians, and the Samnites, and later against overseas rivals like Carthage, Macedonia, and Pontus. Rome's military setbacks during the seven and a half centuries between her founding and the destruction of Varro's legions by the Germans at the Battle of Teutoburg Forest in 9 A.D. were few and memorable. They included the sacking of Rome by the Gauls in about 390 B.C.; the humiliation under the Samnite yoke at Caudine Forks in 321 B.C. (which was speedily avenged by an overwhelming Roman reprisal); the setbacks against Pyrrhus, king of Epirus, and against Hannibal, the great Carthaginian general; the challenge of Mithridates, king of Pontus; Spartacus' short-lived slave revolt; and the slaughter of Crassus and his legions by the Parthians in 53 B.C. at Carrhae.

For the most part, though, Roman military history is a dreary catalog of one-sided battles with outmatched and poorly orga-

3

nized foes, of the destruction or absorption of entire nations into the expanding Roman state, and of almost superhuman resilience in rebounding from rare defeats that would have broken the back of any other nation — such as the disaster at Cannae in 216 B.C., where Hannibal's forces cut down the flower of Rome's entire military.

Political Strength

Nevertheless, the astonishing rise of the Romans was not due wholly or even mostly to their military successes. In their evolution from armed camp to monarchy to republic to empire, the Romans discovered a formula for limiting the power of government by dividing it among several different magistrates and elected bodies. The Roman Republic also developed a written code of laws that defined and protected the rights of Roman citizens.

The exquisitely balanced Roman state conferred an extraordinary degree of political stability, while granting to Roman citizens a degree of personal liberty almost unknown in human history before that time. The Roman state was, wrote Polybius, "a union which is strong enough to withstand all emergencies, so that it is impossible to find a better form of constitution than this."

Many of the institutions of the Roman republican government, as well as the roots of the distinctive Roman culture, developed well before the founding of the republic itself. The Senate, Rome's oldest government body, was apparently founded by Romulus himself. It may have been patterned after the Gerousia, a governing body of Sparta. It also resembled the Athenian Areopagus.

Rome's second king, Numa Pompilius — a Sabine statesman who refused an offer of the kingship until a large body of his fellow citizens persuaded him to accept — set about civilizing the Romans and abolishing the crude despotism of his predecessor. "The first thing he did at the entrance into government," Plutarch relates, "was to dismiss the band of three hundred men which had been Romulus' life-guard ... saying that he would not distrust those who put confidence in him; nor rule over a people that distrusted him."

Numa forbade the use of any graven image in the worship of God, a practice that seems to have persisted for more than a century after his death. He instituted many other religious reforms, including the creation of the Vestal Virgins — a group of virgin priestesses who tended the sacred fire in the temple of Vesta, the goddess of the hearth — and lived a life of conspicuous piety that many of his subjects were pleased to imitate.

Numa was by disposition a man of peace, and wanted to reduce the Romans' love of violence and warfare. He instituted the order of the Fetials, a college of priests whose special task it was, in Plutarch's words, to "put a stop to disputes by conference and by speech; for it was not allowable to take up arms until they had declared all hopes of accommodation to be at an end." The Fetials endured until the late Roman Empire, providing a check of sorts on the power of the Roman state to go to war.

Rome triumphant: The pageantry of a Roman military triumph was a common sight in the streets of ancient Rome. The Roman Republic, almost incessantly at war, became the most formidable military power the world had ever seen.

During his reign, at least, Numa appears to have been successful in taming the warlike disposition of his people, even if it was seldom tamed thereafter. It was the custom in Rome to shut the doors of the temple of the god Janus during times of peace, a custom that, after Numa, was put into practice only once — during the consulship of Marcus Atilius and Titus Manlius in the third century B.C. — in all of the centuries leading up to the reign of Caesar Augustus. Of Numa's rare achievement of peace, Plutarch wrote with admiration:

> During the reign of Numa, those gates were never seen open a single day, but continued constantly shut for a space of forty-three years together, such an entire and universal cessation of war existed. For not only had the people of Rome itself been softened and charmed into a peaceful temper by the just and mild rule of a pacific prince, but even the neighboring cities, as if some salubrious and gentle air had blown from Rome upon them, began to experience a change of feeling, and partook in the general longing for the sweets of peace and order.... For during the whole reign of Numa, there was neither war, nor sedition, nor innovation in the state, nor any envy or ill-will to his person, nor plot or conspiracy from views of ambition.

Kings and Despots

Unfortunately, this state of affairs did not outlive Numa himself. Tullus Hostilius, his immediate successor, was, according to Livy, "not only unlike the preceding king, but was even of a more warlike disposition than Romulus.... Thinking, therefore, that the state was becoming languid through quiet, he everywhere sought for pretexts for stirring up war." Before long, he succeeded in provoking a war with the Albans, a closely related neighboring nation. The war ended with the Roman destruction of Alba — and the permanent enmity towards Rome of Alba's allies.

After the Alban conflict, Tullus declared war against the Sabines, which resulted in a speedy Roman victory. The reign of Tullus, which lasted 32 years, was applauded by Livy for its "great military renown." It set the pattern, to be followed by Rome ever after, of incessant warfare with her neighbors coupled with aggressive territorial expansion.

The four kings that followed Tullus continued the Roman tradition of endless war, with campaigns against formidable foes like the Veii, the Aequans, and the Volscians. The latter two in particular fought the Romans for generations before finally being vanquished and absorbed into the burgeoning Roman state.

Reluctant king: Numa Pompilius, Rome's second and greatest king, at first refused the offer of kingship. His reign was the most peaceful period in Rome's history, and was marked by many religious reforms.

The last king of early Rome, Lucius Tarquinius Superbus ("Tarquin the Proud"), was a vicious despot who came to power by murdering his predecessor, the aged monarch Servius Tullius. Tarquin is said to have been aided in his misdeed by Tullius' daughter Tullia, with whom he had developed an adulterous liaison. Tullia found her father's lifeless body in the street outside the Senate where Tarquin had personally cast it, whereupon she triumphantly drove her chariot over it. According to Livy, she even carried off a portion of her father's remains to be offered up to her household gods.

Tarquin lost no time clamping down on the Roman state. He purged the government of suspected rivals, including many senior senators, and even had a number of his own relatives murdered. He surrounded himself with an armed entourage, since, in Livy's estimation, "he had no claim to the kingdom except by force, inasmuch as he reigned without either the order of the people or the sanction of the senate." Like most tyrants, Tarquin was preoccupied with war and with building monuments to himself, most notably an immense temple dedicated to Jupiter — the Roman god of thunder and skies — intended to be the most magnificent building in the ancient world.

Rise of the Republic

Tarquin's downfall was as dramatic as his seizure of power. His youngest son Sextus developed an illicit passion for Lucretia, the wife of a Roman aristocrat related to Tarquin himself. While Lucretia's husband was away, Sextus crept into her chamber and violated her at the point of a sword. Lucretia immediately sent for her father and husband, requesting each to bring a trustworthy friend. Accordingly, her father brought Publius Valerius, and her husband summoned Lucius Junius Brutus, who happened to be a disaffected nephew of Tarquin. The distraught Lucretia informed the four men what had happened and, as an affirmation of her testimony, committed suicide on the spot, after securing their promise that the guilty party would suffer for his crime.

It was Brutus who drew Lucretia's dagger from the self-inflicted wound, and, holding it aloft, reputedly said: "By this blood, most pure before the pollution of royal villainy, I swear, and I call upon you, O gods, to witness my oath that I shall pursue Lucius Tarquin the Proud, his wicked wife, and all their race with fire, sword, and all other means in my power; nor shall I ever suffer them or any other to reign at Rome." He next led the other three in

Roman soldier of the First Class

the same oath. The four men then bore Lucretia's body to the Forum, where they raised a revolt against the Tarquins. After a 25-year reign of terror, Tarquin the Proud was expelled from Rome, and Brutus and Collatinus, Lucretia's husband, were elected Rome's first consuls.

Lucius Junius Brutus is thus remembered as the father of the Roman Republic. After the expulsion of the Tarquins, he and all Rome took an oath never to allow another king to reign over Rome. The new state, called a "res publica" ("people's thing") in Latin, was something new: a form of government that protected the rights of its citizens while being itself limited by laws and by the diffusion of its powers into many different magistrates and governing bodies. Brutus' commitment to the new republic was so unshakable that he even presided over the execution of several of his own sons and nephews after finding them guilty of conspiring with agents of the exiled Tarquin to reinstall the monarchy. He eventually perished on the battlefield in hand-to-hand combat with the son of Tarquinius Superbus, during one of several unsuccessful attempts by the Tarquins to reconquer Rome.

Roman soldier of the Second Class

Brutus' fellow consul Collatinus, who bore the surname Tarquinius, soon left office and voluntarily went into exile, to allay any fears that another with the name of Tarquin might usurp power. His place was taken by Publius Valerius, the other witness to Lucretia's sui-

9

cide, and usually reckoned along with Lucius Brutus as Rome's most important founding father.

Plutarch compared Publius Valerius, afterwards nicknamed Poplicola ("lover of the people"), to Solon, the great lawgiver of Athens. Indeed, Publius proved to be more of a statesman than his erstwhile colleague Brutus, while being just as strong a supporter of popular liberty. When Publius heard, for example, that some had criticized him for his stately house on a hill overlooking the Forum, he ordered the house pulled down, and moved in with friends until he received a more modest house of his own.

Publius also made substantial reforms in Roman law to shore up the new republican government and to fortify the rights of the people against encroachments by the state. He appointed 164 new senators to fill the vacancies of those purged by Tarquin. He enacted a law permitting offenders convicted by the consuls to appeal their sentences directly to the people, a device that, by depending on the doubtful ability of the masses to deliberate, was probably much less effective as a check on state power than it was intended to be. Publius also instituted the death penalty for usurping any public office without the people's consent and provided for tax relief for the very poor.

Such measures may smack more of democratic excess than of true republican government. Indeed, while Rome eventually achieved the best-balanced form of government in the ancient world and deserved the appellation of republic, she shared with most other ancient popular states the deficiency of allowing the masses to assemble and deliberate directly. In the long run, this handicap, because of the instability it encouraged, helped to doom the Roman Republic. But it must be borne in mind that, when Western civilization was in its infancy, any degree of popular government was probably a distinct improvement over the suffocating despotism that held the rest of the human race in thrall.

With the career and reforms of Publius Valerius — whose name in a latter age was used by American Founding Fathers James Madison, Alexander Hamilton, and John Jay, the authors of *The Federalist Papers*, as an enlightened pseudonym — the Roman Republic was off to a brilliant beginning. Poplicola, after successfully leading Rome in a series of wars instigated mostly by the vindictive Tarquins, stepped down from the consulship

Rome on the ropes: The sacking of Rome by the Gauls circa 390 B.C. was a rare instance of Roman military defeat, and the only time the Eternal City was breached by a foreign military invader until the last years of the empire in the Fifth Century A.D.

and died, having lived a life that "so far as human life may be, had been full of all that is good and honorable," in Plutarch's admiring terminology. But the Roman Republic was to outlive its founders by many centuries, and its legacy by millennia.

CHAPTER 2

THE REPUBLIC MATURES

The Roman Republic was not built in a day, but was the product of generations of reform and even some serious reverses.

About 15 years after the founding of the Roman Republic in 509 B.C., an apparition appeared one day in the Roman Forum. It was no phantom or divine portent, though, but a flesh-and-blood figure, a pale and emaciated old man dressed in rags who soon attracted a large crowd of curious onlookers. Displaying a chest covered with battle scars, the wild-haired old man announced that he had fought bravely for Rome during the war with the Sabines. Then, to gasps of indignation, he displayed his back to his audience. It was covered with hideous scars and wounds, some of them very recent, from tortures received in debtors' prison.

The Roman Forum: Even the ruins of Rome's political and social hub still display fragments of the majesty of the Eternal City in her prime.

He had, he explained to the onlookers, been deprived of his livelihood. Having served in many wars, he was unable to cultivate his lands. Enemy armies had burned his property and driven away his cattle. Worse still, he had been assessed crippling taxes, which he could only pay by taking on heavy debt. As a result, he had lost his property and had been delivered to "a house of correction and a place of execution" as punishment.

The man's story was by no means unusual. Rome, despite having ousted the cruel Etruscan monarch Tarquin the Proud, remained an oligarchic state ruled by the patricians, the Roman aristocracy. The plebeians, or underclass, were disenfranchised, with little representation in Roman government (all senators and consuls were patricians), but provided the bulk of Rome's military forces. Most plebeians depended for their livelihood on farming, an activity that was frequently disrupted by warfare. Moreover, the new lands annexed by Rome as spoils of war were invariably parceled out to patricians, widening the gap between the urban gentry, who controlled the machinery of state and exploited the laws to amass more and more wealth, and the rural underclass, who were systematically divested of their landholdings by war, debt, and heavy taxes.

Discontent and Reforms

Popular resentment boiled over that day in the Forum, as the wretched old man's testimony reminded the assembled masses of the injustices of Rome's class-based system of government. Before long, Rome was in complete turmoil, as angry mobs demanded political representation and even threatened to assassinate the consuls. The Roman Republic, in spite of its many strengths, had serious flaws that only drastic reforms could mend.

Soon, the exasperated plebeians emigrated en masse from Rome to a nearby mountain in what has come to be known as the First Plebeian Secession. They demanded more active representation in the republican government, and were rewarded with the creation of the office of the tribune, a special magistrate who represented the plebeians.

There were originally two tribunes, but more were added with the passage of time. The tribunes held veto power over the laws, elections, and actions of all magistrates except dictators, who in the Roman Republic were appointed for six-month spans to lead Rome through extreme military crises.

Unfortunately, another cause of plebeian discontent, the inequity of property laws, particularly regarding newly acquired territory, was never adequately addressed. An early attempt at a so-called "agrarian law," which would reform the division of public land, was attempted by a consul named Spurius Cassius. His proposal was blocked by patrician influence, however, and Cassius himself was eventually tried and executed for alleged treason. During the later history of the republic, the absence of a just "agrarian law" resurfaced periodically. Eventually, during the administrations of the Gracchi brothers in the second century B.C., this contentious issue became the spark that lit the fuse leading to a long series of civil wars — wars that ended with the rise of the Caesars.

The Need for Written Laws

Even with the tribunes in place, the plebeians chafed under another form of legal abuse. Rome had no body of written laws. Therefore, the patricians, the self-anointed guardians of Roman law, interpreted the law however they saw fit — and always with their own class interests in mind. The plebeians, demanding equal representation under the law, pressed for a written legal code that could be read and understood by all.

In response to pressure for a code of written laws, the Senate, in about 450 B.C., sent a commission of three men to Greece to study the Greek legal code, particularly the laws devised by Solon, the great Greek statesman and lawgiver. The Romans then appointed a council of 10 men, the Decemvirs, who were charged with producing a body of laws that would protect the rights of the Roman people, laws that would be inscribed in stone and remain unchanged. After much deliberation, the Decemvirs produced the famed Twelve Tables of Roman Law.

The Twelve Tables are sometimes characterized as a Roman

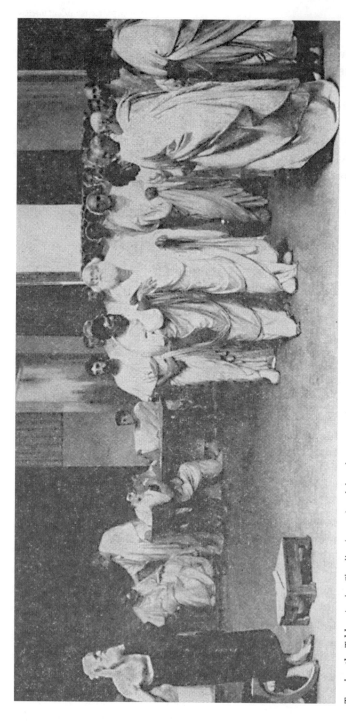

Turning the Tables: Appius Claudius (center) and the other Decemvirs were appointed by the Senate to produce a written law code for Rome. They produced the celebrated Twelve Tables to protect the rights of Roman citizens, but, refusing to relinquish power once the task was finished, became despots themselves.

constitution. However, they had far more in common with ancient legal codes like the Code of Hammurabi and the law books of ancient Israel than with modern written constitutions like the U.S. Constitution. The Twelve Tables were a code of civil laws that protected the rights of citizens rather than defining the powers and offices of the Roman state.

From a modern perspective, those portions of the Twelve Tables that have come down to us are something of a mixed bag. On the one hand, the Tables gave debtors certain protections, such as a 30-day grace period to pay debts (Table III) and provisions against capital punishment without conviction (Table IX). On the other, the Tables required the killing of deformed infants (Table IV), prescribed the death penalty for slander and "giving false witness" (Table VIII), and forbade marriage between patricians and plebeians (Table XI). But with the creation of a written code of laws, which were engraved on 12 stone tablets and kept in the Forum, the Roman Republic was solidified. The Twelve Tables became, like the English Magna Charta, a tangible symbol of Roman liberty, and they served as an effective restraint on the arbitrary interpretation of Roman law.

From Lawgivers to Despots

The story of the Decemvirs, however, did not end with the creation of the Twelve Tables. Led by the charismatic and ambitious Appius Claudius, the Decemvirs refused to step down and attempted to usurp government power. They managed to curry favor with many young patricians and hired some of them as personal military escorts. Thus protected, they were impervious to popular threats. Senators and plebeians alike found themselves under the decemviral yoke. Despite the persecutions, many plebeians took great satisfaction in the Decemvirs' treatment of prominent patricians, while others looked in vain to the patricians for leadership against the new oppressors. "Liberty," wrote Livy, "was now deplored as lost forever; nor did any champion stand forth, or appear likely to do so."

As with the crisis under Tarquin the Proud, Rome's salvation came as a result of the abuse of a woman. In this case, Appius

Claudius developed a consuming lust for a certain virtuous plebeian maiden named Virginia. After failing to seduce the young woman with bribes and other inducements, Appius turned to violence. He attempted to have Virginia seized and enslaved, provoking a hue and cry among the commons.

At first Icilius, Virginia's husband-to-be, tried to reason with Appius: "Though you have taken from us the aid of our tribunes, and the power of appeal to the commons of Rome, the two bulwarks for maintaining our liberty," Icilius protested, "absolute dominion has not, therefore, been given to you over our wives and children. Vent your fury on our backs and necks; let chastity at least be secure." Virginius, Virginia's father, was summoned home in haste from the front, where he found the machinery of tyranny moving relentlessly against his innocent daughter. Appius was preparing to seize Virginia by force in the Forum, when Virginius confronted him. "To Icilius, and

Innocent blood: The persecution of the virtuous Virginia by the Decemvir-turned-despot Appius Claudius led her father to take her life to save her from rape and slavery. The shocking event incited the Romans to rise up and overthrow the tyrannical Decemvirs.

not to you, Appius, have I betrothed my daughter," he told the smirking Decemvir, "and for matrimony, not prostitution, have I brought her up. Do you wish men to gratify their lust promiscuously like cattle and wild beasts? Whether these persons will endure such things, I know not; I hope that those will not who have arms in their hands."

At this implied threat, Appius ordered his men to disperse the crowd protecting Virginia. In despair, her father asked if he might have a moment alone with his daughter before delivering her into bondage. Seizing a knife, he stabbed his daughter to death, crying, "In this one way, the only one in my power, do I secure to you your liberty." Virginius himself then led a revolt that overthrew the Decemvirs. Appius was thrown into prison, where he took his own life, and Roman liberty was restored.

Both the expulsion of the Tarquins and the overthrow of the Decemvirs were prompted by attacks on Roman women. For this reason, these two episodes were often held up by later historians as evidence of the moral rectitude of the early Roman Republic. The dissolute Empire of later centuries, which Juvenal famously condemned for its addiction to "bread and circuses," placed no such premium on chastity, feminine or otherwise. But the early Romans, if the stories of Lucretia and Virginia are to be believed, valued the honor of their women so highly that they were willing to defy tyrants to preserve it.

A Moral Society

Moral strength, in fact, has to be accounted one of the reasons for Rome's rise to greatness. While the Romans lacked some of the civilizing virtues introduced by Christianity, there can be no question that, in contrast with most of their contemporaries, the Romans were a moral people, renowned for their honorable dealings even with enemies, and zealous upholders of family values.

Such a society tends to produce outstanding leaders, and early Rome was no exception. Marcus Furius Camillus, sometimes called the "Second Founder of Rome," epitomized the virtuous heroism of the Roman Republic at its peak. Camillus first earned renown by successfully storming the city of the Veii, which the Romans had been besieging for 10 years. His next success came against the Faliscans at the siege of the well-fortified city of Falerii. According to tradition, a certain schoolmaster inside Falerii used his influence to trick a group of schoolchildren into following him outside the city walls. There he delivered them into the hands of the Romans, with the suggestion that they be used as hostages to persuade the people of Falerii to surrender.

When the Falerian traitor was brought to Camillus, the latter was, according to Plutarch, "astounded at the treachery of the act, and, turning to the standers-by, observed that 'war, indeed, is of necessity attended with much injustice and violence! Certain laws, however, all good men observe even in war itself, nor is victory so great an object as to induce us to incur for its sake obligations for base and impious acts. A great general should rely on his own virtue, and not on other men's vices.'" Having rebuked the man, Camillus had him stripped and bound with ropes, and ordered rods and scourges to be given to the children. The children then drove their treasonous schoolmaster back to the city, where the astonished citizens, having already discovered the disappearance of their children, expected the worst. When their children were returned to them unharmed and the traitor in their midst delivered up for punishment, they counseled together and decided to surrender to Camillus, confident that they could trust the character of a man who adhered to such high moral standards even in wartime.

Camillus paid a severe price for his principled actions at Falerii. His soldiers were indignant at being denied the spoils from a city that had surrendered voluntarily, and many of Rome's citizens were disappointed at losing the opportunity to oust the inhabitants of the great city and resettle it themselves, as had been the usual Roman custom with conquered cities. In consequence, Camillus found himself the target of a political smear campaign and finally decided to go into exile.

Not long after Camillus left Rome, the Gauls, led by Brennus, occupied and sacked the city of Rome in about 390 B.C.

Their capture of the city was accompanied by a fearful slaughter in which men, women, and children were indiscriminately put to the sword. The desperate senators barricaded themselves inside the Capitol and sent word to Camillus, begging him to return and save the city from the Gallic marauders. Camillus accepted the appointment of dictator, raised a military force, and destroyed the host of Gauls almost to a man.

Camillus led several other noteworthy military campaigns against such perennial foes as the Volscians and the Aequans, and continued active in public affairs into old age, until finally succumbing to the plague during an epidemic.

Scipio Africanus: The most illustrious of the Scipios, Africanus earned his title by leading Roman forces to victory against Hannibal and his Carthaginians in the decisive Battle of Zama in North Africa. His military prowess aside, Scipio was noted for his upright character.

For his selfless devotion to the republic, his unshakable integrity, and his judgment as a military leader, Camillus exemplified the principled soldier-statesmen who led the republic to greatness during its best years.

Rome's greatest strength was her ability to produce men of the caliber of Camillus. As late as the Second Punic War in the late third century B.C., when Rome was already building an overseas empire, Scipio (later surnamed Africanus), another great military leader, had taken possession of the bride-to-be of an Iberian prince named Allucius. The girl had been captured by Scipio's forces during his siege of Cartagena, a Carthaginian stronghold in Spain. The beautiful girl was brought before Scipio as a prize, but the great general refused to gratify himself

21

at her expense. Instead, Allucius himself was brought before Scipio and assured that his future wife had not been mistreated in any way by his men. "This only reward I bargain for in return for the service I have rendered you," he told the grateful young prince, "that you would be a friend to the Roman people; and if you believe that I am a true man,... that you would feel assured that in the Roman state there are many like us; and that no nation in the world at the present time can be mentioned ... with which you would rather be in friendship."

The greatness of Rome was a reflection of the greatness of her people. In an altogether different age, when the might of ancient Rome was already distant history, another sovereign, John Cantacuzenus, one of the last rulers of Byzantium — the site of modern-day Istanbul — contemplating the imminent ruin of his people, observed:

> There is nothing more conducive to the destruction of a nation ... than the lack of men of wisdom or intellect. When a republic has many citizens ... of high quality it quickly recovers from those losses that are brought about by misfortune. When such men are lacking, it falls into the very depths of disgrace.

As long as the Roman Republic produced men and women of integrity, its vitality was assured. Rome remained nearly impervious to external military threat, and avoided the scourge of civil war and other debilitating internal crises. On the rare occasions when Rome saw her freedom threatened by external or internal threats, she always displayed resourcefulness and resiliency. Only when later Romans succumbed to moral depravity did Rome cease to produce leaders of the caliber of Camillus, Poplicola, and Scipio. Only then did she become easy prey to foreign military powers; only then was she wracked with unending civil unrest.

CHAPTER 3

THE IMPERIAL REPUBLIC

Once a republic reluctant to fight wars except in self-defense, Rome became an imperial colossus capable of annihilating an entire nation out of sheer spite.

In all of human history, there have been few spectacles to rival the great battles of the ancient world, with their pageantry, color, and awful carnage. And few battles of that age could match the drama that unfolded under the hot Italian sun one August morning in 216 B.C. near Cannae during the Second Punic War. On that fateful day, two of the mightiest armies ever assembled faced each other for what was to be a cataclysmic showdown. On one side was arrayed almost the entire military force of Rome: eight full legions, amounting to more than 80,000 men. On the other were the forces of Carthage, led by the matchless Hannibal, the greatest adversary Rome had ever faced.

With dazzling speed, Hannibal had led his vast army out of Spain, across southern Gaul, and over the Alps into Italy before Rome even realized he had left the Iberian peninsula. Hannibal's army quickly inflicted two crushing defeats on Roman forces, at Trebia and Lake Trasimene. For a time, the Romans adopted a policy of containment, avoiding direct battle with Hannibal while harassing his forces and attacking his supply lines. But Rome soon tired of permitting Hannibal to ravage Italy uncontested, and resolved to risk all in a single battle. Hannibal's forces, especially his celebrated elephants, had been depleted by the arduous trek over the Alps and the subsequent campaigning. But they were still formidable, numbering around 50,000 men, including expert cavalrymen from Numidia in North Africa and slingers from the Balearic Islands.

Amidst the din of trumpets and of battle cries, the two massive forces charged across the dusty battlefield of Cannae, the respective infantries flanked on either side by crack cavalry units. As the lines crashed together, the Romans, who had deployed extra infantry in the center of the formation in hopes of breaking through the Carthaginian lines, found themselves outflanked by elite North African cavalry units. Hannibal's cavalry

Hannibal Crossing the Alps: In one of the most brilliant and unconventional maneuvers in military history, the Carthaginian leader Hannibal led his forces, complete with war elephants, across the Alps into Italy. Thousands of his men and nearly all of the elephants were lost in transit, but Hannibal still won many victories over Rome in the Italian heartland.

overwhelmed the Roman cavalry on both flanks and then swept behind the Roman forces to attack from the rear. In short order, the Romans were completely hemmed in by the Carthaginians. Hannibal's numerically inferior forces then slaughtered practically all of the Romans on the field.

When the choking dust of battle subsided, more than 70,000 Romans lay dead on the fields of Cannae, including one consul and at least two former consuls, not to mention most of the rest of Rome's land forces. Ten thousand more, who had been left to guard the Roman camp, were taken prisoner by the victorious Carthaginians, who themselves had lost just 6,000 men. Only 3,000 Romans escaped Cannae alive. By all appearances, Rome was doomed. The brilliant and apparently invincible Carthaginian general had virtually wiped out Rome's military forces in a single stroke, and the road to the city of Rome itself now lay undefended.

How could such a tragedy come to pass? In the fairly recent past, Rome had successfully fended off the challenge of another military genius, Pyrrhus, the king of Epirus, a kingdom in southwest Greece. Rome's leader at Cannae, Lucius Aemilius Paulus, had earned distinction in successful campaigns in Illyricum (in the approximate area of modern Albania). In the First Punic War, the Romans had soundly beaten the Carthaginians, leaving Rome in possession of the island of Sicily and with significant alliances and interests elsewhere.

Now an upstart general with an unconventional, multinational force had invaded the Roman heartland and had struck a blow from which no reasonable observer could expect Rome to recover. Hannibal Barca was tutoring Rome in the costs of empire. His massive invasion force was showing Rome by brute experience that imperial expansion has a high price.

Rome had never been a peaceful state. In the early centuries of the republic, however, many of Rome's conflicts were provoked by jealous neighbors like the Volscians and the Aequans. The early Italian peninsula was a tough neighborhood, with rival Etruscan and Latin states, including Rome, jostling for control, and the Gauls, who occupied parts of northern Italy, frequently making incursions southward. Enclaves of southern Italy, called Magna Graeca, or "Greater Greece," were Greek. Though conflict was frequent among all of these jostling ethnic groups, many of Rome's early campaigns against her peninsular neighbors were defensive, not expansionist.

A dispute with the Greek city of Tarentum in southern Italy gave Rome her first taste of conflict with an overseas power. The Tarentines requested the aid of Pyrrhus, who sailed with his forces across the Adriatic and defeated the Romans in two costly battles, Heraclea and Asculum. In a later campaign, Rome finally defeated Pyrrhus at the Battle of Beneventum, but was content to expel him from Italy, rather than to seek reprisals on Greek territory.

A Fateful Choice

The situation was far different a decade or so later in 264 B.C., when Rome decided to intervene militarily in a conflict on the island of Sicily. The powerful Greek city of Syracuse had besieged the city of Messina, which was occupied by an unsavory band of Italian mercenaries called the Mamertines. The Mamertines frequently plundered surrounding territories, as bandits are wont to do, until Syracuse grew weary of their depredations. The Mamertines, in turn, called upon *both* Rome and Carthage for help. Initially only Carthage jumped into the fray, but then Rome — against her better judgment, and rationalizing that she needed to act as a counterpoise against Carthage's occupation of Messina — jumped in as well. For the first time ever, Rome sent a large expeditionary force overseas, and soon found herself directly confronting the Carthaginians for control of Messina and the rest of Sicily. Thus began the first of the three Punic Wars between Rome and Carthage.

The First Punic War, one of the costliest in recorded history up to that time, lasted for 23 years. Because it was primarily a naval conflict, the Carthaginians, with their vast navy and experience with sea warfare, enjoyed a heavy advantage. Nevertheless, the Romans soon built a navy of their own, designing their craft after captured Carthaginian vessels, and before long, the tide of the war began to change. Rome enjoyed a substantial constitutional advantage over Carthage, because the old, oligarchic Carthaginian state could not match the vitality of Rome's comparatively open society and competitive marketplace. Rome failed in her attempt to conquer Carthage by land, but ultimately won the war at sea, forcing Carthage's army stranded on Sicily to surrender.

The First Punic War exhausted both Rome and Carthage for a generation, but it had kindled in Rome a fatal yearning for conquest. No longer content to mind her own affairs in Italy, Rome began to see herself as the mistress of the Mediterranean. Besides governing her new Sicilian territory, Rome sought to dictate terms to Carthage at the far western end of the Mediterranean, in Iberia. There, Rome ordered the Carthaginians to keep their forces south of the Ebro River. When the impetuous young Carthaginian general Hannibal flouted Rome's dictate in 218 B.C., Rome declared war against Carthage for a second time.

The Second Punic War was shorter than the earlier conflict, but its 16 years exacted a far heavier toll on both sides than the first. Hannibal, according to Roman accounts, had sworn an oath to fight Rome all his life and, unlike many of Carthage's dissolute nobility, possessed the resolve and the military genius to do so. After leading his army across the Alps into Italy, he won three monumental victories against the Romans culminating in the debacle at Cannae, victories that laid the Eternal City itself bare for conquest.

Fortunately for Rome, in one of history's more enduring mysteries, Hannibal chose not to follow his crushing victory at Cannae with an immediate assault on the Roman capital, but instead resumed his campaigning in Italy, seeking allies among the fickle Roman tributary cities. Some, like Tarentum and Syracuse, declared themselves for Hannibal and later incurred the wrath of Rome. Though Syracuse was defended by the ingenious war machines designed by still-famous scientist and inventor Archimedes, it fell to the Romans after a two-year siege. Tarentum became a focal point of the war in Italy, with

27

control over the city changing hands several times between Rome and Carthage.

The Second Punic War produced its share of Roman leaders — among them Fabius Maximus, whose careful delaying tactics kept Hannibal at bay where direct confrontation could not, and Marcus Claudius Marcellus, whose forces took Syracuse. But Rome's champion, and the central figure of the age, was Publius Cornelius Scipio, afterwards named Africanus.

Scipio's Defiance

Several of Scipio's relatives had died in war against Carthage, and Scipio himself was one of the few to escape the carnage at Cannae. Young Scipio had, therefore, a very keen appreciation of the potency of the Carthaginian military. He volunteered to lead Roman forces against a portion of Carthage's forces who were stationed in Iberia and, despite his youth, his demeanor so impressed the Senate that he was given the command. Scipio was as good as his word, and after his forces had defeated the Carthaginians in Spain, he was hailed as a hero.

Yet Scipio, for all his brilliance as a leader, orator, and military strategist, was also a man of boundless personal ambition. He wanted to achieve greater glory by leading Roman forces into Africa and taking the war to Carthage itself. Only such a bold move, he argued, would induce Hannibal, who was still making trouble in Italy, to vacate the Roman heartland and return to defend his own borders.

Many senators, led by the now-venerable Fabius Maximus, opposed Scipio's plan. Besides the additional cost in men and materiel, the pitfalls of further overseas expansion troubled their republican instincts. Scipio, however, made it very clear that he would ignore Senate authority and appeal directly to the people, if need be, to secure approval for the invasion.

In an epic Senate debate recorded by Livy, Fabius reproved his younger colleague for being more interested in personal glory than in wise policy. Hannibal, Fabius pointed out, was still in Italy; did it not make better sense to undertake the less glamorous task of defending the Italian homeland than to seek glory and conquest overseas? "Although you naturally prize more highly the renown which you have acquired than that which you hope for," he told young Scipio, "yet surely you would not boast more of having freed Spain from war than of having freed Italy.... Why then do you not apply yourself to this, and carry the war in a straightforward manner to the place where Hannibal is...? Let there be peace in Italy before war in Africa; and let us be free from fear ourselves before we bring it upon others." Concluding his address, Fabius added witheringly, "Publius Scipio was elected consul for the service of the state and of us, and not to forward his own individual interest; and the armies were enlisted for the protection of the city and of Italy, and not for the consuls, like kings, to carry into whatever part of the world they please from motives of vanity."

In reply, Scipio reminded the senators that he had lost his father and uncle to Carthaginian arms, and admitted that he did indeed seek greater glory — an instinct that he considered natural and noble. The Senate, having already been informed of Scipio's intent to bypass their authority, was unimpressed. Quintus Fulvius, a former consul, bluntly asked Scipio to declare openly to the Senate whether "he submitted to the fathers to decide respecting the provinces, and whether he intended to abide by their determination, or to put it to the people." Leaving no doubt of his intentions, Scipio responded boldly that "he would act as he thought for the interest of the state," in Livy's words.

Scipio's defiance was the first time in the history of the republic — though not, unhappily, the last — when a charismatic, successful military leader placed his own judgment above the laws of Rome and the counsels of the Senate. The Senate, fearing a confrontation, eventually authorized Scipio to cross into Africa, giving the color of legality to the young general's challenge. But his impudence set a gloomy precedent, one that Rome would bitterly regret in generations to come — when military leaders less principled than Scipio would not scruple to trample underfoot the will of the Senate and the people alike.

Scipio successfully invaded Carthaginian territories in North

Africa and won a resounding victory at Zama over Hannibal's hastily recalled forces, ending the Second Punic War. The city of Carthage itself was left intact, but the terms of the Roman victory denied the Carthaginians all but a token military and reduced her to a tributary nation. Hannibal himself, wily as ever, managed to elude capture and flee to Syria, where he took refuge with King Antiochus and played a significant role in stirring up that potentate to make war with Rome.

War Without End

The third century B.C. closed with Rome in control of all of the former dominions of Carthage save a few portions of North Africa and the city itself. Having secured the western Mediterranean territories as Roman dominions, Rome now turned her attentions to the east, where the Greek city-states were in turmoil, threatened both by a resurgent Sparta under the despot Nabis and by ambitious Macedonian rulers seeking to establish hegemony over the Hellenic world. Now acclimated to her role as Mediterranean policeman, Rome sent troops to Greece to quell the ambitions of Nabis, justifying every step of the expedition as a mission to liberate the Greeks.

After defeating Nabis and his Macedonian allies, the Roman general Titus Quinctius made a dramatic announcement at Corinth to the effect that Rome, having restored to the Greeks the freedom that was their birthright, would now withdraw all her forces to Italy. The rumormongers were wrong, he claimed, who "had spread the calumny that the cause of liberty had been wrongly entrusted to the Roman people, and that the Greeks had merely exchanged Macedonian masters for Roman lords." He laid down strong recommendations for how the Greeks should conduct their affairs in the future, and enjoined them to "guard and preserve [their liberty] by their own watchfulness, so that the Roman people might be assured that liberty had been given to men who deserved it, and that their boon had been well-bestowed." According to Livy, the source of this account, "the delegates listened to these words as if to a father's voice, and tears of joy trickled from every eye." The servile Greeks watched with

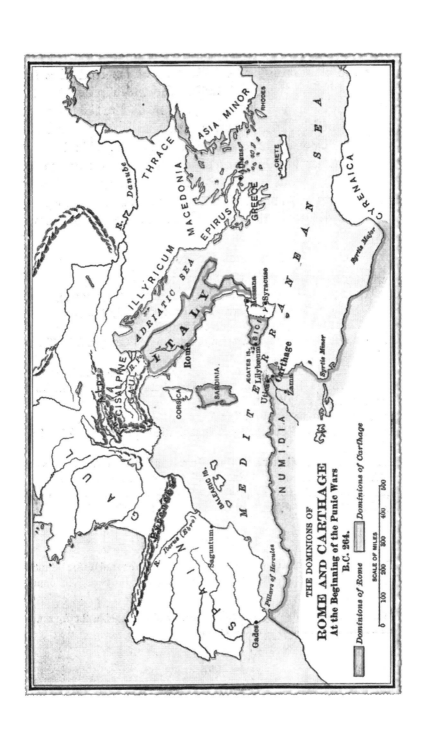

THE DOMINIONS OF
ROME AND CARTHAGE
At the Beginning of the Punic Wars
B.C. 264.

SCALE OF MILES

0   100   200   300   400   500

Dominions of Rome   Dominions of Carthage

enthusiasm as, in 194 B.C., the Romans, as good as their word, evacuated their forces from Greek territory.

Unfortunately for Greece, independence was short-lived. Within a few years, Antiochus of Syria, egged on by the vindictive Hannibal, declared war on Rome and sought allies among the Greeks. In the complex wars that followed, the Roman military returned to Greece to fight Antiochus and his Greek allies, and then became embroiled in several decades of war in the eastern Mediterranean, primarily against the kings of Macedonia, that left Rome in permanent control of Greece by about 167 B.C.

During the first half of the second century B.C., Rome was not only conquering the eastern Mediterranean, but was also constantly at war in Iberia and in North Africa. One particularly noteworthy conflict, the so-called Lusitanian War, which took place in the second half of the second century B.C., was typical of the sordid wars of conquest Rome was now willing to embark upon. A Roman consul named Servus Sulpicius Galba, a Roman commander in Iberia (modern Spain and Portugal), encountered resistance from a tribe known as the Lusitanians, who are believed to have been the ancestors of the modern-day Portuguese. The Lusitanians agreed to lay down their arms and settle on lands Galba designated for them, but were then indiscriminately massacred by the perfidious Romans.

A Lusitanian named Viriathus, who escaped the massacre, led a guerrilla war against Rome. The Romans, unable to find a general capable of defeating Viriathus, suffered a series of severe military setbacks against the Lusitanians. Finally, a general named Marcus Pompilius Lenas decided to use treachery again, and bribed three Lusitanian envoys to assassinate Viriathus, a deed which, once accomplished, finally led to the subjugation of the Lusitanian people. Instead of receiving the promised reward, the three Lusitanian turncoats were executed by the Romans, who self-righteously declared, "Rome does not pay traitors." Such treacherous tactics, once disdained by moral leaders like Camillus, became par for the course for a Rome now eager to expand her dominions by any means necessary.

While preserving the political forms of the old republic, Rome was transforming into an empire in substance. Her vast new conquered territories, with their unruly citizenries, alien cultures, and harsh, far-flung geography, would pose greater and greater administrative challenges to the Roman state. The republic, after all, was designed to govern Romans within a single cohesive territory; her constitution was not well adapted to the suppression of multinational imperial subjects.

Social Decay

At home, too, the character of Roman society was beginning to change. The Romans began to develop a taste for luxury and grew contemptuous of the austere virtues of earlier times. In 186 B.C., Rome was shocked by an unprecedented calamity that signalized the moral dry rot consuming Roman society.

The crisis began with the arrival in Italy of a mysterious Greek who claimed to be an initiate of a secret cult dedicated to Bacchus, the god of wine and transgressive behavior. The cult, with its secret nighttime orgies, human sacrifices, and other abominable practices, spread rapidly among the Romans. The adherents of Bacchus aimed not merely to corrupt Roman morals, but also to undermine the Roman government, according to the consul Spurius Postumius, who first exposed the conspiracy before the Roman Senate. "Never," exclaimed Postumius, "has there been so much wickedness in this commonwealth, never wickedness affecting so many people, nor manifesting itself in so many ways.... And they have not yet put into practice all the crimes towards which they have conspired. Their impious conspiracy still confines itself to private outrages, because it has not yet strength enough to overthrow the state. But the evil grows with every passing day.... It aims at the supreme power in the state."

In response to Postumius' warnings, the Bacchic cult was broken up, its shrines destroyed, and many of its adherents imprisoned or executed. For the time being, the fabric of Roman society was kept from unraveling; but as the very potency of the Bacchic cult showed, it was starting to fray around the edges.

Carthage's Last Stand

With the Roman conquest of the Mediterranean all but assured by the middle of the second century B.C., only one lingering challenge lay yet unresolved — Carthage. After Carthage's total defeat in the Second Punic War, the Carthaginians, who were first and foremost a commercial, not a military, republic, rebounded economically. Seemingly content to prosper commercially under the Roman military yoke, the Carthaginians strove to keep the onerous obligations of their treaty with Rome. Unfortunately for them, the Roman lust for vengeance had not yet been satisfied.

A large number of Roman politicians viewed the resurgence of Carthage as an unacceptable challenge and agitated for a resumption of hostilities. Their mouthpiece was the senator Cato the Elder, whose condemnation of Carthage was so intense that he ended every speech with the famous phrase "Carthago delenda est" ("Carthage must be destroyed"). Rome would not rest until she found a pretext for eliminating Carthage. Massinissa, the king of Numidia, finally gave her one.

The Numidians, a rival African power, had long been at odds with the Carthaginians, their former allies. When Massinissa began taking advantage of Carthaginian military weakness and attacked Carthaginian towns (with the support of Rome), the Carthaginians, unable to rely on protection from Rome, raised their own military and defended themselves.

This was all the pretext that Rome needed. Frothing senators, led by Cato, pointed to the developing new Carthaginian armed forces as an intolerable threat to Rome. The Carthaginians were put on notice that they could expect a Roman invasion and utter desolation unless they submitted to Roman terms. The supine Carthaginians sent envoys to Rome to plead their case, but found themselves confronted by a hostile united front of Roman leadership already resolved upon war. With treachery more reminiscent of the smirking despots Rome had overthrown in nobler times, the Roman senators, holding out false promises of peace, deliberately misled the Carthaginians into surrendering hostages and armaments to Rome.

Death of a republic, rise of an empire: It could be argued that two republics died in spring of 146 B.C., when Roman forces, resolved on a program of imperial conquest, stormed and destroyed Carthage, a centuries-old citadel of Mediterranean trade and culture.

Even after a huge Roman expeditionary force had crossed into Africa, Carthage was still suing for peace. But it was not to be. The Romans finally showed their hand by deliberately demanding what even the terrified Carthaginians could not accept: evacuating their city and moving inland, where they would be resettled. Rome would demolish the city itself, to ensure that it could never be a threat again.

In dismay, the Carthaginians resolved to fight their implacable enemy. The merciless Roman forces laid siege to the great city of Carthage, wonder of the Mediterranean for an entire age. The Carthaginians proved astonishingly resilient in their final struggle. Though they had been beguiled by Rome into destroying their navy and giving up their weapons, they managed to construct new ships and weapons using resources within the walls of their own city. The entire city worked night and day manufacturing weapons out of any available objects. All metal was melted down to be converted into spear and arrow tips and swords. Even women's hair was cut off and braided into cords for catapults.

The desperate Carthaginians enjoyed several military successes against Rome, but they could not break the siege. Finally, after two years of stalemate, Rome appointed Scipio Aemilianus, the adopted grandson of Africanus, as the leader of the forces besieging Carthage.

Under Scipio's energetic, ruthless generalship, the war was soon resolved. As the Carthaginian defenses collapsed, 50,000 of her citizens surrendered to the Romans under a promise of leniency. Their lives were spared, but they were eventually sold into slavery. The remaining inhabitants of the city, numbering as many as 650,000, were less fortunate.

The Romans systematically slaughtered all the Carthaginians, including women and children, an event that may have been the worst butchery of civilians the world saw before the 20th century. It is said that Scipio Aemilianus shed tears of regret as he witnessed the destruction of Carthage, but that did not stop him from allowing his men to massacre the inhabitants. He then razed the entire city to the ground in a final act of fanatical vindictiveness that even the barbarians who sacked Rome in later centuries never equaled.

Such was the moral decline of Rome, from a republic that fought wars almost exclusively in self-defense to a belligerent, self-absorbed colossus capable of annihilating an entire nation out of sheer spite. For Rome had become an imperial republic; her chief concern now was not securing the liberty of her own citizens, but the domination of foreign powers. But Rome was soon to learn an awful lesson: imperial republics are inherently unstable. They must either abandon their designs of conquest and domination abroad, or modify their domestic policies to better conform to a program of imperial administration — and renounce liberty into the bargain.

Scipio, as he watched the flames consume Carthage, reportedly likened the scene to the destruction of Troy and wondered aloud whether a similar fate would befall Rome. As events turned out, the Roman Republic would not outlive fallen Carthage by many generations. Rome, having sown the wind abroad, before many years would reap the whirlwind at home.

CHAPTER 4

RISE OF THE
WELFARE-WARFARE STATE

The death throes of the once-great Roman Republic begun when its leadership embarked on militarism and exploited class envy to consolidate power.

Mob rule: In one of Rome's first experiences with civil unrest, Caius Gracchus, demagogue and would-be reformer, flees from a murderous mob. Like his older brother Tiberius, Caius proposed unwise solutions to long-standing social grievances — and paid the ultimate price at the hands of bloodthirsty partisans.

The man sped down the Capitoline Hill from the Roman Senate, fleeing from a bloodthirsty mob. At a wooden bridge several of his companions urged him to run on, while they defended the narrow way. He raced through the streets of Rome, calling loudly for help. Throngs of onlookers cheered encouragingly as he passed, but no one offered to help. He pleaded with curious bystanders to lend him a horse to escape his pursuers, but to no avail.

As the relentless pursuit drew close, the man, together with his most trusted servant, slipped into a sacred grove consecrated to the Furies. Realizing that escape was impossible, he ordered his servant to cut his throat to spare him the indignity of execution by the mob. The rabid partisans soon found his lifeless body alongside that of the faithful servant, who had turned his dagger on himself after carrying out his master's last wish. Triumphantly, they severed the dead man's head and carried it off to claim a reward in gold. The man's headless body, along

Failed reforms: The Gracchi brothers proposed to rectify unjust Roman property laws by forcible land redistribution, which inflamed rather than mollified partisan passions.

with those of thousands of his followers who had been killed in the unrest, was dumped in the Tiber River. The unfortunate victim of the mob's wrath was Caius Gracchus, and the year was 121 B.C., just 25 years after the destruction of Carthage.

The spasm of civil violence was not Rome's first. Just 11 years earlier, Caius' older brother Tiberius Gracchus and many of his supporters had suffered a similar fate in what was acknowledged to be the first civil violence in Rome. In both instances, the controversy had arisen over a centuries-old injustice: the unequal recognition of property rights under Roman law, and the perceived need for some kind of land redistribution, known to the Romans as an "agrarian law."

One of Rome's greatest strengths had always been her unity. With the exception of the treason of a Roman general named Coriolanus and his defection to Rome's sworn enemies, the Volscians, centuries before, Rome had always managed to solve her internal disputes without resort to violence or betrayal. Even episodes of plebeian unrest, such as the First Plebeian Secession, had always been settled through peaceful compromise. But with the tumult under the Gracchi, the waning Roman Republic entered a new, more perilous stage of decline, in which demagogues incited civil unrest with welfare-state programs, and a new generation of ambitious politician-generals began to covet absolute power.

Class Warfare

While Rome was assembling her overseas empire, various problems, both civil and constitutional, continued to fester at home. Foremost among them was the growing disparity between the wealthy patricians on the one hand and the masses of plebeians and slaves on the other. Slavery in ancient Rome was not, as practiced more recently in Europe and the United States, solely or even primarily dependent on imported chattels from conquered lands. It was part of Roman civil law: parents under certain circumstances could sell their children into slavery, and desperate citizens sometimes even sold themselves into slavery to avoid debts and other problems.

41

Because of Rome's long-standing practice of granting or sell-ing real estate acquired through conquest to certain powerful patrician families, the wealthy few became wealthier still, while the numbers of the enslaved swelled. "The rich," explained the historian Appian, "gained possession of most of the undistribut-ed land.... They used persuasion or force to buy or seize property which adjoined their own, or any other smallholdings belonging to poor men, and came to operate great ranches instead of single farms. They employed slave hands and shepherds in the estates to avoid having free men dragged off to serve in the army, and they derived great profit from this form of ownership too, as the slaves had many children and no liability to military service and their numbers increased freely. For these reasons the pow-erful were becoming extremely rich, and the number of slaves in the country was reaching large proportions, while the Ital-ian people were suffering from depopulation and a shortage of men, worn down as they were by poverty and taxes and military service." Romans, in other words, were losing their livelihood to armies of slaves on vast estates, while enduring higher and higher taxes and the ravages of endless war.

For these ills, the Gracchi offered an equally unpalatable solution: confiscating land from Rome's wealthy classes and forcibly redistributing it among the poor. The first, Tiberius, while serving as a plebeian tribune, successfully pushed for an agrarian law stipulating that no landowner should hold more than 500 jugera (one Roman jugerum equaled roughly 5/8 of an acre). Under Tiberius' measure, the state would buy back from the landowners those holdings of land exceeding this limit, and would redistribute them among the poor. Three men, or trium-virs, would oversee the redistribution; they were to be Tiberius Gracchus himself, his younger brother Caius, and his father-in-law Appius Claudius.

Not surprisingly, the wealthy bitterly opposed Tiberius' agrarian law. His colleague, the tribune Octavius, went so far as to veto the measure to prevent it from being passed. Tiberius Gracchus, however, declaring that no tribune was qualified for office who was unwilling to carry out the will of the people in support of his bill, illegally ousted his rival. The bill was then passed by the Assembly, but was denied funding by the Senate, which controlled the purse strings of the Roman government.

Tiberius Gracchus then tried to usurp the Senate's prerogative by seizing monies bequeathed to Rome by a wealthy king, in order to fund his agrarian reform bill. He flouted Roman tradition by seeking reelection the following year, in spite of a long-standing custom that prohibited the same man from holding the office twice in succession. This was enough for the senators and their patrician support base. On the day of the election, Gracchus appeared in the Forum with an armed entourage. Violence broke out, led by the senator Scipio Nasica, and Gracchus and several hundred supporters were killed.

A decade later, history repeated itself in the tragic career of the younger Gracchus, Caius. Caius revived his brother's land redistribution scheme, and added to it a multitude of other leveling measures, such as price controls on grain. Like Tiberius, Caius also ran for successive terms as tribune. He too found himself the target of patrician wrath and met an untimely end, along with up to 3,000 of his backers.

The civil unrest associated with the Gracchi brothers is usually regarded as the beginning of Rome's long spiral into civil war and Caesarism. The actions of the Gracchi and of their opponents set yet another perilous precedent, that political differences could be resolved by using the power of mob violence to override the law. Before the time of the Gracchi, assassinations had been unknown in Rome; after their time, they quickly became routine.

After the defeat of Carthage, Rome's overseas expansion continued. In North Africa and in Iberia, Roman forces met with constant resistance and several significant setbacks. The Iberians were finally subdued, after decades of warfare, with the fall of the city of Numantia in 133 B.C. Conflict in Africa, however, was never to be completely resolved, and one African war in particular — the Jugurthine War — though relatively insignificant in terms of Roman lives and materiel lost, did incalculable long-term damage to the Roman state because it set the stage for the rise of the first Roman despots.

The Rise of Militarism

Jugurtha was a renegade king of Numidia, an important North African nation that at various times had been an important ally both of Carthage and of Rome. Numidia's greatest monarch, Massinissa, had been a Roman ally in the Second Punic War, but his illegitimate grandson Jugurtha, after killing off a rival heir, incurred the enmity of Rome by seeking to enlarge his inherited kingdom and by killing some Roman merchants in the process. Though not a particularly gifted military tactician, Jugurtha was a master of intrigue and managed to keep the Romans off-balance with a mixture of well-placed bribes and feigned compliance.

In 112 B.C., however, war finally broke out, and for several years Jugurtha, taking advantage of the desert terrain, the harsh climate, and the mobility of his lightly armed forces, managed to fend off the Roman military. After five years, however, Rome appointed a new consul, Caius Marius, whose name, along with that of his right-hand man and eventual rival Lucius Sulla, was to become a hiss and a byword for future generations of Romans.

Marius changed the makeup of Rome's military by turning the former all-civilian corps into professional volunteers. Moreover, whereas property ownership had formerly been a requirement for Roman soldiers, Marius' reforms led to the recruitment of vast numbers of poor, landless plebeians whose prospects could be enhanced if land were redistributed to them. This encouraged tension between the military and the Senate, most of whose members opposed land redistribution. It was also a strong incentive for Rome's new professional soldiery to be less loyal to the far-away Roman government than to the military leaders under whom they served.

The deadly rivalry that grew up between Marius and Sulla, that would eventually lead to civil war, began in the Jugurthine conflict. When Jugurtha was eventually captured by the Romans after being betrayed by an unreliable ally, both men claimed credit for his defeat, but soon patched up their public differences.

Marius' stock with the Roman people rose still further during

Despot-in-waiting: Caius Marius, distinguished Roman military leader in wars against Jugurtha, the Cimbri, and the Teutones, reclines against the ruins of Carthage. Marius, by later introducing Rome to the horrors of despotism, started Rome down the same road that fallen Carthage had followed.

the Cimbrian War with the Cimbri and Teutones, two ferocious German tribes that invaded Gaul in 109 B.C. They inflicted a catastrophic defeat on Roman forces at Arausio (now Orange in southern France) in 105 B.C., wiping out two entire armies totaling as many as 110,000 men, many of whom had been pinned against a river. This, the worst Roman defeat since Cannae, opened the way for the first Germanic invasion of Italy in 102 B.C., but Marius proved equal to the challenge. He dealt first with the Teutones and their allies at Aquae Sextiae (now Aix-en-Provence) as they marched towards the Alps in what is now southeast France.

The battle cost up to 100,000 lives. The forces of the Teutones were wiped out. The victorious Marius then turned his attention to the Cimbri, who had managed to penetrate northern Italy. In a decisive encounter at Vercellae, his forces slaughtered more than 140,000 Germans, ending the German threat for several generations.

The numbers of battle dead in the Cimbrian War are truly staggering, even to the modern mind. In a single war consisting mostly of three major battles, more than 300,000 men perished, an astonishing figure when the smaller populations in Europe of that day are taken into account. In the second half of the second century B.C. alone, Roman dominions had been the setting for bloodshed and slaughter on a scale seldom seen, much less surpassed, in human history. The Third Punic War had cost as many as three-quarters of a million lives, while wars in Iberia and North Africa had claimed many tens of thousands more. Rome's wars were becoming bigger, bloodier, and more frequent, and her adversaries more and more determined. At the same time, Roman forces became more and more ruthless, giving little quarter and asking none.

But worse was yet to come. In the turbulent, blood-soaked first century B.C. that would see the final end of the republic, the fearsome Roman armed forces, with their formidable discipline and awesome military machines, would be turned upon Rome herself and visit on the Roman people the same horrors that they had become accustomed to inflict upon the rest of the world.

Enclosed is our
special thank you for your
recent contribution to
The John Birch Society

CHAPTER 5

CIVIL WAR AND DESPOTISM

Plagued by murderous ambition, Rome's politician-generals turned their armies against each other — and even against Rome herself.

Travelers passing along Rome's Appian Way between Capua and Rome in the spring of 71 B.C. were greeted by a gruesome sight. For mile after mile along the road, festering bodies hung from crucifixes as kites, jackdaws, and other carrion birds picked at the remains. More than 6,000 men had been brutally

Routing the rebellion: In 71 B.C., Roman troops led by General Crassus defeated an army of rebel slaves led by the former gladiator, Spartacus. Thousands of the captured rebels were nailed to crosses alongside the Appian Way; their lifeless and rotting bodies were displayed for years thereafter as a warning to other would-be rebels.

47

put to death along Rome's main thoroughfare. They were not common criminals but captured soldiers of a former gladiator named Spartacus, who had led a damaging revolt against the Roman government.

Defeated by Crassus, one of Rome's iron generals, thousands of Spartacan rebels had been publicly executed as a salutary lesson to others contemplating rebellion against the Roman state. The bodies were never removed, but hung on their grisly scaffolds for years thereafter, a grim and poignant reminder of the monstrous regime taking shape in the heart of what had once been the world's freest civilization. In 71 B.C., the mass executions along the Appian Way were only the latest in a series of horrors that Rome had endured during nearly two decades of civil war and despotic government. No doubt some of the older passersby, who remembered Rome in better days, gazed on the fly-blown victims of the latest convulsion and wondered: how had the republic come to this?

The First Civil War

It began with the so-called Social War, which erupted in 91 B.C. At issue was a long-standing sore spot among the non-Roman Italian peoples living under Roman rule. For centuries, Rome had been absorbing other Italian peoples into the republic, but had never granted them Roman citizenship. When a consul named Drusus, who had been pushing to extend citizenship to non-Roman Italians, was assassinated, the Italian cities formed a league and revolted against Rome. Tens of thousands of Romans and Italians died in three years of brutal war — in which Marius and Sulla, two of Rome's most prominent military leaders, became bitter political enemies. The war ended when Rome negotiated a settlement granting citizenship to non-rebellious Italians and to those rebels who laid down their arms.

In the meantime, another threat to Rome had arisen in the east, in the person of the formidable Mithridates VI, the king of Pontus, a powerful state in Asia Minor. Mithridates was a prototypical oriental despot, having come to power by murdering most of his siblings and marrying his own sister. He is said to have spoken 25 languages and to have spent years building immunity to every kind of poison then known. He possessed a huge, well-equipped army and navy. Having territorial ambitions of his own in Asia Minor and the Aegean, Mithridates detested Roman power and the high-handed way in which the Romans presumed to dictate terms to every other nation. In 88 B.C., as the Social War was petering out in Italy, Mithridates decided to make his move against Rome.

In that year, Mithridates' agents instigated a massacre of all Romans living in Asia Minor. The victims, numbering in the tens of thousands, included merchants and diplomatic envoys as well as their families. After such a catastrophe, Rome had little choice but to declare war on Mithridates, an enterprise that promised to be Rome's greatest military exploit since the Second Punic War.

Rome's First Despots

With such a prospect for personal glory, the rivalry between Marius and Sulla, which had simmered since the Jugurthine War more than a decade earlier, exploded into the open. Sulla, serving as one of Rome's consuls, was chosen to lead the campaign against Mithridates. Marius, seething with envy but having no legal recourse, allied himself with the newly enfranchised Italian citizens of Rome. He encouraged them to vote for a new law giving him command over the Mithridatic task force.

Furious, Sulla decided to use the troops under his command to unseat Marius before turning his attention to Mithridates. Although many of his officers resigned in protest, his foot soldiers, eager for the spoils of war in the East once Marius was out of the way, followed their leader in a fateful march on Rome. Sulla was met along the way by several deputations, who asked him why he was marching against his native land under arms. His reply, shameless and unwavering, was the rationale of usurpers in every age: "To free her from tyrants." As his troops swept into Rome, they encountered only light resistance from the Marians, and large-scale butchery was averted — for the time being. Marius himself slipped out of the city and escaped

49

to Africa, intending to regroup and return. Sulla meanwhile lost no time in reforming the Roman constitution in his favor, which included installing several hundred new senators and diminishing the power of the tribunes, who since the days of the Gracchi, Rome's first full-blown demagogues, had been exercising unconstitutional, demagogic power.

His reforms, though long overdue, had been instituted by force of arms, setting Rome on a path toward despotism from which recovery was increasingly unlikely. "This was," noted Appian gloomily, "the first army composed of Roman citizens to attack their own country as though it were a hostile power. From this point onwards their conflicts continued to be settled by military means and there were frequent attacks on Rome, and sieges, and every sort of incident of war, because nothing remained, neither law, nor political institutions, nor patriotism, that could induce any sense of shame in the men of violence."

After having a number of prominent Marians killed, Sulla, anxious to leave the seething capital, took his army and departed for Asia Minor. There, in what became known as the First Mithridatic War, he eventually forced Mithridates to capitulate. In less than three years, Sulla's forces killed more than 160,000 of the enemy and recovered Greek and Asian territories annexed by Mithridates. The monarch of Pontus himself, however, was allowed to live on and to rule over his original domains because Sulla had run out of time. During his absence, Marius had returned to Rome and had instigated a reign of terror.

Proscriptions and Pogroms

Sulla had left as his consular successor in Rome a man named Cinna, who soon allied himself with the Marians and with the voting bloc of new Italian citizens. In a showdown with the other consul, Octavius, who represented the Senate and the interests of the old citizenry, Cinna was defeated, divested of his consular office, and chased from the capital city, whereupon he began inciting neighboring cities to rebellion. He soon raised an army and returned to encamp outside of Rome. The Roman consuls summoned an army of their own and encamped nearby,

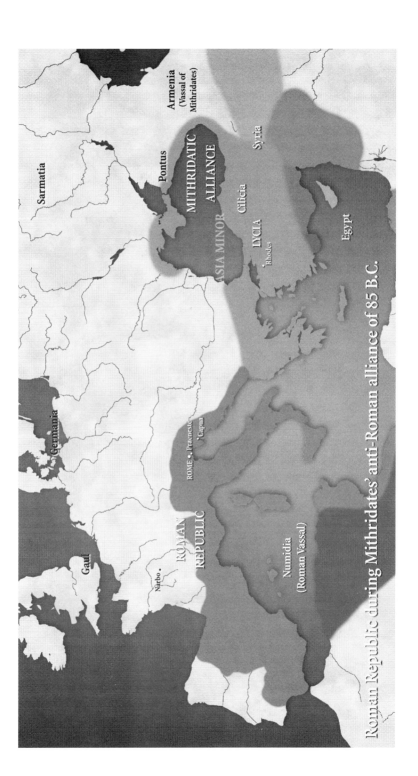

Roman Republic during Mithridates' anti-Roman alliance of 85 B.C.

Sulla's fateful march: Decades before Julius Caesar crossed the Rubicon, General Sulla invaded Rome. "This was the first army composed of Roman citizens to attack their own country as though it were a hostile power," recorded the historian Appian. Sulla's march inaugurated a tragic era of civil war and despotism.

while the city waited fearfully for what was sure to be a dreadful outcome. The fugitive Marius seized this opportunity to return from Africa, and using his past military exploits as a sales pitch, quickly raised yet another army and marched to Rome to join forces with Cinna.

The Marian forces cut off Rome's food supplies. The Senate, seeing that conditions were hopeless, negotiated the surrender of Rome on condition that Marius would not perpetrate a massacre. As the terms of surrender were accepted, records a somber Appian, "Marius, standing beside the consular stool, said not a word but made it plain by the savagery of his expression what murder he would unleash."

No sooner were Cinna and Marius ushered into Rome by the cowed citizens than an orgy of bloodletting was unleashed the likes of which Rome had never witnessed nor could have imagined. All political enemies of Marius were cruelly put to the sword, and the heads of slain senators, consuls, and praetors were put on public exhibit in the forum. "No one," says Appian, "was permitted to give any of the dead burial, and birds and dogs tore apart the bodies of such distinguished men. There were many further unauthorized and uninvestigated murders carried out by the rival parties.... All [Sulla's] friends were put to death, his house was razed to the ground, his property was declared forfeit, and he was proclaimed an enemy of the state."

Marius died before he could be reelected consul, but Cinna remained in power with another longtime confederate, Carbo. Cinna was then assassinated by a mob of unruly soldiers, leaving Carbo in sole command of Rome.

In the midst of this bloody tumult, Sulla returned from the East, bent on retaliation for the Marian outrages. He quickly attracted many allies, including the able general Metellus, who had been busy stamping out the last remnants of the Social War, and a young general named Gnaeus Pompeius, or Pompey, who raised three legions in support of Sulla. With these forces, Sulla for the second time marched toward Rome.

This time, the consular forces, led by Carbo and Marius, the son of the late despot, engaged Sulla's forces in a number of battles across Italy and overseas. The conflict escalated into an epic civil war that claimed many tens of thousands of Roman lives in Italy, Africa, and even Spain. Sulla's generals won a string of victories against the Marians and committed wide-scale atrocities in many conquered cities. When Praeneste fell, for instance, thousands of her citizens were put to the sword. Similar reprisals were carried out elsewhere.

Sulla finally entered Rome and launched a fearful bloodbath there as well, massacring dozens of senators and thousands of noblemen. "He was so terrible and quick to anger in every-thing," wrote Appian, "that he killed Quintus Lucretius Ofella [a former friend] in the open forum.... After this, Sulla called the people to an assembly and said: 'Understand this, my friends, and hear it from my own lips: I killed Lucretius because he would not obey me.' And he told them a story: 'A farmer who was plowing was being bitten by lice. Twice,' he said, 'he let go of the plough and shook out his tunic; but when he was bitten again, he burnt the tunic so as not to keep wasting time. So I advise people who have been defeated twice not to ask for incineration the third time.' With these words, then, Sulla reinforced their terror, and ruled them as he pleased." Even Plutarch, so often the eulogist, had little good to say about Sulla's character:

> In general he would seem to have been of a very irregu-lar character, full of inconsistencies with himself; much given to rapine, to prodigality yet more; in promoting or disgracing whom he pleased, alike unaccountable; cringing to those he stood in need of, and domineering over others who stood in need of him, so that it was hard to tell whether his own nature had more in it of pride or of servility.

He was also, Plutarch tells us, shamelessly immoral, consorting with dissolute entertainers night and day. His riotous lifestyle brought about physical as well as moral deterioration. He was afflicted by a "creeping sickness" that saw his flesh corrupted by an unknown cause and his entire body literally eaten alive by lice.

Before meeting such a horrible end, Sulla had abdicated his dictatorial power — the only Roman despot ever to do so. A deceptive calm settled over Italy, although the civil war persisted for several more years in distant Spain before the last remnants of the Marian forces were finally annihilated. In the year of Sulla's death, 78 B.C., the purges had subsided, Mithridates had been placated, and tenuous threads of legality still held the Roman Republic together.

But forces were already in motion that could not be stopped. Mithridates would soon rise again, providing political opportunity for the ambitious young general, Pompey. The Spartacan revolt would do the same for Crassus. Yet another military prodigy, Julius Caesar, who had already distinguished himself in various Asian campaigns, was in Rhodes studying the art of rhetoric and persuasion, preparing for a political career.

In the space of only a few decades, the Roman Republic had descended swiftly from irresponsible demagoguery to full-blown despotism, and from militarism overseas to civil war at home. The decades and wars that yet lay ahead were to produce horrors beside which even the atrocities of Marius and Sulla would pale. But they were also to be a season of tragic heroism, as the final defenders of the old republic — Cato, Cicero, and Brutus — made a magnificent last stand on behalf of Roman civilization and liberty.

CHAPTER 6

CICERO, CATILINE, AND CONSPIRACY

Vying for control, Lucius Catiline conspired to become Rome's monarch, while Cicero worked to expose and thwart his plans and keep Rome's Republic alive.

Sometime in the year 75 B.C., a boat sailed from Italy bound for the island of Rhodes in the eastern Mediterranean. The boat's most important passenger was a 25-year-old Roman advocate, who was sailing with his entourage. The advocate, Caius Julius Caesar, was already well known in the Roman capital for his flowing and persuasive oratory and for having logged a string of successful prosecutions of corrupt governors. The young Caesar was sailing to Rhodes to improve his rhetorical skills under the

Cicero denounces Catiline in the Roman Senate, in Maccari's famous rendition. Cicero was Rome's greatest statesman and orator, as well as a formidable man of letters (many of his voluminous letters, speeches, and commentaries have come down to us). He proved more than a match for the conspiratorial cunning of Catiline.

tutelage of the legendary Appolonius Molo, a noted philosopher and rhetorician.

Julius Caesar was not Appolonius' only pupil of note. Another young Roman, Marcus Tullius Cicero, also spent significant time with the master rhetorician at about the same time. Appolonius, it is said, spoke no Latin, but he was so impressed with both Cicero's command of Greek and with the young man's rhetorical ability that he allegedly told him: "You have my praise and admiration, Cicero, and Greece my pity and commiseration, since those arts and that eloquence which are the only glories that remain to her, will now be transferred by you to Rome." True to the prediction of the old Greek scholar, Cicero became Rome's greatest orator, as well as her greatest statesman and man of letters — and an able foil for the rising ambitions of Julius Caesar and his confederates.

In the wake of the dictatorship of Sulla, other ambitious men besides Julius Caesar were jostling for power in Rome. Licinius Crassus, the vanquisher of Spartacus and reputed to be Rome's wealthiest citizen, was one of them. Gnaeus Pompeius, also known as Pompey, was another. Pompey had been an able military leader for the Sullan forces and cemented his reputation with the destruction of the Cilician pirates in 67 B.C. But in the years between 70 and 60 B.C., the greatest threat to the republic came not from charismatic generals but from a subtler source — a clever, amoral intriguer who formed a conspiracy to overthrow the republic.

Master of Deceit

Lucius Catiline was a dissolute patrician and senator gifted with good looks, intelligence, boundless energy, and tremendous personal magnetism. Catiline could, the historian Sallust (and Catiline's contemporary) tells us, "endure hunger, cold, and want of sleep to an incredible extent. His mind was daring, crafty, and versatile, capable of any pretense and dissimulation. A man of flaming passions, he was as covetous of other men's possessions as he was prodigal of his own.... His monstrous ambition hankered continually after things

Conspiracy unmasked: Some of the leaders of the Catilinarian conspiracy are brought before the Senate, under Cicero's orders, to be tried for treason and sedition.

extravagant, impossible, beyond his reach."

Disaffected with republican government and determined to replace it with a monarchy, Catiline formed a secret society to prepare for a revolution. In morally decrepit Rome, he had no trouble attracting a following. Sallust informs us: "Amid the corruption of the great city Catiline could easily surround himself, as with a bodyguard, with gangs of profligates and criminals. Debauchees, adulterers, and gamblers, who had squandered their inheritances in gaming-dens, pot-houses, and brothels; anyone who had bankrupted himself to buy impunity for his infamous or criminal acts; men convicted anywhere of murder or sacrilege, or living in fear of conviction; cut-throats and perjurers, too, who made a trade of bearing false witness or shedding the blood of fellow citizens; in short, all who were in disgrace or afflicted by poverty or consciousness of guilt, were Catiline's intimate associates."

Catiline specialized in corrupting youth, procuring mistresses for them, encouraging the practice of unnatural vice, and even training them in the art of forging documents. He enlisted many veterans of the Sullan dictatorship in his movement, men who had expended their spoils since the death of their leader and wished to renew the despotism which had once rewarded them.

Never had the Roman state been so ripe for overthrow. In addition to declining moral standards, Rome was bankrupt. Italy had been emptied of most of her military forces, including their strongest leader, Pompey, who was fighting a second war against a rejuvenated Mithridates. Many of Rome's political leaders, including Crassus, Pompey's bitter rival, were aware of and sympathetic with Catiline's designs. Catiline, having assembled a considerable following throughout Italy, as well as a core of confidants in the Senate, began organizing and training his recruits, preparing for an armed overthrow of the republic. Only one man stood between Catiline and his goal of absolute power: Cicero.

Defender of the Republic
In 63 B.C., Cicero defeated Catiline in the consular election, and the latter immediately began plotting Cicero's demise. He

sent a band of assassins to Cicero's house, but Cicero, having been warned that his life was in danger, barricaded himself inside and frustrated the plot. In spite of these events, however, it appears that Cicero had not yet learned the full extent of Catiline's conspiracy. Nevertheless, Cicero did deliver, on November 8, the first of four orations in opposition to Catiline in the Senate. According to Sallust's version of events (which does not agree with Cicero's), Catiline sat in smug silence as the great Roman orator heaped invective on him. When Cicero sat down, Catiline rose to defend himself. He invoked his high birth

Rome's rivals: Gallic warriors as they probably appeared in the first century B.C. Catiline's conspirators tried to enlist the help of Gallic tribes living under Roman rule in Italy to support the planned overthrow of the republic.

and his years of public service; how could anyone, he asked, take the word of this upstart immigrant (Cicero was a native of Arpinium, about 70 miles from Rome) against that of a patrician like himself?

Cicero's powerful oratory, however, had won many allies. The entire Senate shouted down Catiline, calling him an enemy and a traitor. At this unexpected reversal, Catiline became enraged. "Since I am encompassed by foes," he thundered, "and hounded to desperation, I will check the fire that threatens to consume me by pulling everything down about your ears." Saying this, he stormed out of the Senate and fled from Rome — but not before leaving instructions with his most trusted confidants, led by Cethegus and Lentulus, to "do everything possible to increase the strength of their party, to find an early opportunity of assassinating Cicero, and to make arrangements for massacre, fire-raising, and other violent outrages." He promised them that he would soon return to Rome — at the head of a large army.

Pompey the Great: Rome's greatest military leader in Cicero's time, Pompey vanquished the Cilician pirates and Mithridates, king of Pontus, before subduing Palestine.

Catiline's agents busied themselves with final preparations for what was shaping up to be a meticulously planned and remarkably sophisticated revolution. Many of Catiline's corrupted youthful confederates were instructed to murder their fathers, even as 12 conflagrations were to be kindled at picked spots across Rome. Catiline's emissaries fanned out across Roman territories in Italy, seeking allies among non-Roman subject peoples. Some of them, still smarting from the indignities of the Social War, an unsuccessful bid for independence from Rome on the part of various Italian subject states, agreed to support the revolution. But one group betrayed Catiline — the Allobroges, a Gallic tribe whose territory formed the northernmost portion of the Roman province of Transalpine Gaul. The Allobroges themselves had dispatched envoys to Rome to complain of abuses by Roman administrators and of heavy debts. Yet presented with an opportunity to overthrow their overweening masters, the Allobroges hesitated. Considering the vast resources of Rome, defeat was a real possibility, with the reprisals that would inevitably follow. Perhaps they doubted, as well, the good faith of their would-be patron, Lucius Catiline. Whatever the reasons, after considerable debate, it was the Allobroges that dealt Catiline's conspiracy a crippling setback.

There was in Rome a certain Quintus Fabius Sanga, who acted as the Allobroges' patron. It was Sanga whom the Allobroges approached with tidings of the impending revolution and the vast conspiracy behind it. Sanga immediately informed Cicero, who instructed the Allobroges to feign sympathy with the conspirators, in order to find out as much as they could about the organization's membership and plans. They obligingly met with Lentulus, Cethegus, and the other core conspirators and requested sealed, written instructions to carry back to their countrymen. Some of Catiline's men were to accompany the Allobroges back to their homeland. This was communicated to Cicero. The latter arranged to have the party intercepted and arrested, with the understanding that the Allobroges were to be released. Cicero personally interrogated the first detainees and examined their papers. He then ordered the other chief conspirators in Rome, including Lentulus and Cethegus, to be rounded up.

Debate in the Senate

At this point, Cicero faced a dilemma: he was well aware that the conspirators had many allies in the Senate and elsewhere, allies who would make successful prosecution well nigh impossible. He also understood that, if the leaders of the conspiracy were freed, the republic was likely doomed, so pervasive and well organized had Catiline's organization become. The Roman public, upon first learning of the conspiracy and its exposure, "praised Cicero to the skies," in Sallust's words; but partisans of Catiline were still at work sowing discord and shoring up Catiline's support base.

Cicero had the conspirators brought before the Senate in order to discuss how to punish them. Instead of unanimity on the need to rid Rome of the band of detestable traitors, Cicero found to his consternation that the Catilinarians had a powerful senatorial patron who was nearly his equal in eloquence and popularity: Julius Caesar. Both Cicero and his able colleague, Cato the Younger, believed Julius Caesar to be a member of Catiline's band, a belief that was apparently shared by many other contemporaries. The historian Appian also gave some credence to this view, although Sallust — a friend and unabashed partisan of Caesar — did not. Whatever the case, Julius Caesar's actions in the Senate on the conspirators' behalf certainly are more suggestive of trying to help associates than of preserving the republic. "It is not easy to discern the truth," Caesar told his Senate colleagues, "when one's view is obstructed by emotions.... You ... gentlemen must take care that the guilt of Publius Lentulus and the others does not outweigh your sense of what is fitting, and that you do not indulge your resentment at the expense of your reputation." Caesar went on to give a carefully nuanced discourse on the dangers of overreacting and of taking extreme measures without legal coloration. He recommended that, instead of being executed, the conspirators should be deprived of their property and consigned to internal exile in various cities that "are best provided to undertake their custody."

Caesar's calculated rhetoric swayed many in the Senate, but the debate was not finished. Marcus Cato, known to history as Cato the Younger, arose. Reminding his audience that the men before them planned to "make war on their country, parents, altars, and hearths," he observed that mere punishment was not enough: "Other crimes can be punished when they have been committed; but with a crime like this, unless you take measures to prevent its being committed, it is too late: once it has been done, it is useless to invoke the law." He then chided many of the senators for having been "more concerned for your houses, villas, statues, and pictures, than you have for your country." "In heaven's name, men," he urged them, "if you want to keep those cherished possessions, whatever they may be, if you want to have peace and quiet for the enjoyment of your pleasures, wake up while there is still time and lend a hand to defend the Republic. It is not a matter of misappropriated taxes, or wrongs done to subject peoples; it is our liberty and lives that are at stake."

He contrasted for his audience the moral virtues of the old republic with the paralyzing vices of the present era: "They were hard workers at home, just rulers abroad; and to the council-chamber they brought untrammeled minds, neither racked by consciousness of guilt, nor enslaved by passion. We have lost these virtues. We pile up riches for ourselves while the state is bankrupt. We sing the praises of prosperity — and idle away our lives. Good men or bad — it is all one: all the prizes that merit ought to win are carried off by ambitious intriguers. And no wonder, when each of you schemes only for himself, when in your private lives you are slaves to pleasure, and here in the Senate House the tools of money or influence. The result is that when an assault is made upon the Republic, there is no one there to defend it."

Having thus rebuked his colleagues, Cato recommended death for the conspirators. The senators, acclaiming Cato's courage and, according to Sallust, "reproaching one another for their faintheartedness," adopted a resolution to put the conspirators to death. Fearing delay, Cicero directed that they at once be taken to the place of execution deep inside the prison, a filthy, sunless chamber called the Tullianum. There, Cethegus, Lentulus, and three other conspirators were put to death by strangling.

Defeat of Catiline

Catiline himself, however, was still at large with a considerable army. Many of his men deserted when they learned that the conspiracy had been exposed and its leaders executed. Even so, more than a few remained faithful to their leader and joined him in a retreat to a remote, mountainous area near Pistoria, a city in the Tuscany region of northern Italy. Waiting nearby for an opportunity to attack Catiline were several legions under Metellus and Caius Antonius, who cornered Catiline and his army against a range of mountains. Out of options, Catiline decided to risk immediate battle to decide the issue. After a rousing speech, he led his men into combat against the veteran Roman legions. Catiline's men, having resolved to conquer or die, fought savagely and exacted a terrible toll on the government forces. Catiline himself, realizing his cause was lost, decided to die like a Roman and waded into the thick of the affray. His forces were cut down almost entirely, but many Roman soldiers lost their lives as well. Perhaps 20,000 died in the Battle of Pistoria in January of 62 B.C.; Sallust informs us that Catiline's body was found far from the place where his vanguards had fallen, surrounded by the bodies of government soldiers.

For the moment, Rome breathed more easily. A deadly conspiracy had been unmasked and uprooted, though at a high cost in lives. The prestige of Cicero and his able colleague, Cato, had never been higher.

But Crassus and Caesar, both of whom had been sympathetic with, and probable participants in, the Catilinarian conspiracy, were alive and well. Julius Caesar in particular was already regrouping from his failure to save the Catilinarians. He was at once subtler and more charismatic than Catiline. He knew that power lay in forging alliances of convenience, and he began to look to Crassus and Pompey for support.

In addition to Caesar's intrigues, Rome was still beset by economic woes, and the moral turpitude that Cato had condemned was as prevalent as ever. The republic, in spite of the best efforts of Cicero and a dwindling number of republican patriots, was teetering on the brink of collapse. The descent into Caesarism was less than two decades away.

Julius Caesar: The man who gave his name to imperial despotism, Caesar was a gifted orator, writer, and advocate besides being a talented military leader.

CHAPTER 7

THE RISE OF CAESARISM

The weakened Roman Republic was crushed by Julius Caesar, a charismatic military leader who exploited his popularity with a Roman people who desired security above all else.

Adoring fans: Julius Caesar basking in the admiration of his soldiers. Caesar's rise to power owed much to the fierce loyalty of the fighting men who served under him.

The Cilician pirates in the early first century B.C. were the scourge of the eastern Mediterranean. They commanded huge fleets and immense amounts of wealth from their strongholds along the southeast coast of Asia Minor and had spread their depredations over the entire Aegean Sea. By 75 B.C. they apparently enjoyed the sponsorship of Rome's sworn enemy Mithridates, king of Pontus, who, having already lost one debilitating war with Rome, still sought to undermine Roman power any way he could. Sometime in that year, a group of Cilicians captured a vessel carrying a young Roman aristocrat named Julius Caesar.

According to the story, the young Caesar laughed at his captors' demand for a ransom of 20 talents. He told them they had no idea whom they had captured and instructed them to ask for 50 talents instead. The pirates readily agreed to his bold demand, and Caesar dispatched most of his entourage back to Italy to round up the ransom money. In the meantime, Caesar more or less took command of the pirates' camp, insisting on preferential treatment, writing letters and essays, and deriding the illiterate pirates as ignorant savages. He also laughingly promised the pirates that he would crucify every last one of them. The Cilicians, unsure what to make of this cheerful, powerfully built young man with the emotionless eyes, played along with what they assumed were foolish jests by a spoiled socialite who hadn't grasped the full peril of his situation.

After a lapse of little more than a month, Caesar's friends returned with the ransom money, and the Cilician pirates set him free. It was the last mistake they were to make. Julius Caesar went directly to the nearest port, Miletus in Asia Minor, and assembled a small fleet of mercenaries. He then sailed back to the island where his erstwhile captors were still encamped. His forces quickly defeated and captured the pirates, and Caesar ordered them all crucified. However, in a fit of magnanimity to the condemned, he ordered their throats to be cut, to spare them the full agony of death by crucifixion. After all, he reminded them, they had treated him well in captivity.

This was the personality of the man who dominated his age

like no other before or since, saving only One who came into the world a few decades later to preach the coming of a very different kind of kingdom from that espoused by Caesar and his confederates, and who had nothing in common with Julius Caesar except his initials. Gaius Julius Caesar — military genius, charismatic leader of men, author, demagogue, consummate politician — was one of the most contradictory characters ever to occupy the stage of history. He shared Sulla's lust for dominion, but lacked his bloodthirsty vindictiveness. Capable of ruthlessness beyond measure, Caesar also frequently displayed calculated clemency. He understood, where Marius, Sulla, and Cinna had not, that the path to supremacy lay in patronage and flattery, not in pogroms. His personal assets — a keen wit, powerful intellect, decisiveness, and an athletic physique hardened by years of discipline — won him instant allegiance among the men he commanded and allowed him to ingratiate himself with the masses. In an age that produced a constellation of luminaries — Cicero, Brutus, Cato, Pompey, Crassus, and many others — Caesar outshone all the rest. Yet in spite of his extraordinary assets, Julius Caesar was a tragic man who, more than any other Roman leader, was responsible for the downfall of the republic.

Early Life

Caesar was born in 100 B.C. and as a young man married Cornelia Cinnilla, the daughter of Cinna, the leader of the Marian faction. He found himself on the wrong side of Rome's first civil war when the victorious Sulla began his purge of all of Marius' supporters. Caesar fled from Rome and enlisted in the military to campaign in Asia Minor. While there, he is said to have developed an indecent relationship with the king of Bithynia, a powerful kingdom in northern Asia Minor. Homosexuality at the time was still taboo in Rome (in stark contrast to ancient Greece), and Caesar's political enemies were quick to amplify the rumors of Caesar's moral misconduct. In spite of the scandal, Caesar, returning to Rome after Sulla's death, was able to build a creditable career as an advocate and gained a reputation as an unusually powerful and persuasive orator.

Caesar had two great rivals in Rome for power and prestige: one, Pompey, eclipsed him in military exploits and the other, Cicero, in rhetorical skill. Although friends from youth, Pompey and Cicero were completely different in background and temperament. Pompey came from a wealthy, well-connected family, whereas Cicero came from what would now be styled the middle class, lacking the pedigree for automatic promotion and patronage. Pompey, who sided with the Sullan faction in the great civil war that arose between the rival despots Marius and Sulla, was rewarded by the latter with his daughter's hand in marriage. Pompey was only too happy to divorce his first wife to become the Roman dictator's son-in-law. After his marriage, he was dispatched to Sicily to quell the remnants of the Marian resistance there. In Sicily, Pompey earned a reputation as a capable but ruthless military leader noted for his severity in dealing with opposition. Sicily was a major source of Roman grain, and its strategic position in the mid-Mediterranean made it an asset that could not be squandered. "Stop quoting laws," Pompey reputedly told the refractory Sicilians, "we carry weapons."

Following his success in bringing Sicily to heel, Pompey was dispatched to North Africa and eventually to Spain, where the last remnants of the Marians, led by a capable general named Sertorius, held out until 71 B.C. Immediately after his victory in Spain, Pompey returned to Italy in time to assist Crassus in suppressing the uprising of Spartacus — and to lay claim to a piece of the credit for the Roman victory. He was then elected consul for the first time, in 70 B.C.

Pompey's profile grew still further during the next decade. In 67 B.C., in spite of bitter debate in the Senate, Pompey was given unprecedented power — absolute authority over the Mediterranean Sea and all coastal territory extending 50 miles inland — in order to conduct a campaign against the Cilician pirates. The campaign was brief and exterminated the pirates as a military threat. Instead of returning to Rome, however, Pompey departed for Asia Minor, where he helped another general, Lucullus, defeat Mithridates for the second and final time. He

Victors and vanquished: The once-proud Gauls submit to Caesar and the Roman yoke.

then led Roman forces into Armenia, Syria, and Palestine, including Jerusalem itself, all of which he annexed for Rome. He returned to Rome in late 61 B.C. to wild acclaim and a sumptuous two-day triumph in honor of his exploits. His popularity at an all-time high, Pompey's stock rose still higher after several large personal donations to the Roman treasury.

The Road to Power

In the meantime, Caesar's other rival, Cicero, had gotten the better of the Catiline affair, in which a monstrous conspiracy to overthrow the Roman Republic was exposed and dismantled, largely through Cicero's diligence. Caesar, who had defended Catiline's confederates in the Senate, was oratorically worsted by both Cicero and Cato; suspicions of his involvement in the Catilinarian conspiracy tainted him in the eyes of many. By all appearances, in the late 60s, Caesar's star was declining, and those of his rivals were ascending.

Julius Caesar, however, had the good fortune of being consistently underestimated by his enemies. He recognized Pompey and Crassus, two of Rome's wealthiest men and most celebrated military leaders, as indispensable allies. In 59 B.C., Caesar, having managed to get himself elected consul for the first time, forged an informal, semi-secret political alliance with these two men. This, the so-called First Triumvirate, was very much a marriage of convenience. Pompey needed Caesar's political support for his project of conferring state lands on veterans who had served under his command, and Crassus coveted the authority to launch a military expedition against Parthia, a powerful Persian state in Mesopotamia. Pompey and Caesar agreed to set aside their quarrels, and the former even married Caesar's daughter Julia to cement the alliance.

The following year, 58 B.C., Caesar was made proconsul over Roman Gaul, where he promptly launched his famous war of conquest in Gaul and Britain. The Gallic campaigns, generally considered the greatest military feat since the conquests of Alexander the Great, were a turning point in the history of Rome and of the Western world. They not only brought most of what is now France and the Low Countries, as well as a part of Britain, under the Roman yoke, they transformed Caesar into a military hero whose popularity, at least with the masses, eclipsed even that of Pompey.

Caesar, a tireless chronicler of his own exploits, disseminated accounts of his victories over the various Gallic and British tribes. His history, designed to appeal to the general public rather than to the literati, was written in the terse, straightforward language familiar to every second-year Latin student. Caesar's account of his exploits in the Gallic wars electrified the Romans, and the ambitious general's popularity soared.

In addition to his undeniable qualities as both a military leader and rhetorician, Julius Caesar was blessed with extraordinary charisma. Endowed with a hardy physique and uncommon stamina, he earned the slavish devotion of his soldiers through his willingness to share their hardships and risks on the battlefield, often plunging into the thick of combat heedless of mortal danger.

After three years of Caesar's spectacular success in Gaul, Pompey and Crassus, elected consuls in 55 B.C., honored their agreement with him and extended his proconsular authority. They, like many others, appear to have underestimated Caesar and put too much faith in the strength of their alliance with him. But in the years immediately following, fate took a hand in two crucial events that none had foreseen.

The first blow to the Triumvirate was the death of Julia in 54 B.C. Both Caesar and Pompey were heartbroken, and Pompey soon began to have second thoughts about his alliance with Caesar. He spurned Caesar's offer to marry one of his nieces, choosing instead one Cornelia Metella, the daughter of one of Caesar's political enemies.

The following year, catastrophe struck the Roman expeditionary forces in Parthia. Crassus and his son, leading a huge Roman army, allowed themselves to be lured deep into the burning desert by the wily Parthian general Surena, where they were cut off and slaughtered completely. Crassus himself was taken prisoner by the Parthians, where he met a gruesome

No escape: Pompey, shown here fleeing Rome before Caesar's arrival, wanted to avoid bloodshed in the capital city. After nearly defeating Caesar at Dyrrachium, his army was overwhelmed at Pharsalus.

end peculiarly apt for Rome's wealthiest citizen: the Parthians poured molten gold down his throat.

This, the battle of Carrhae, was one of Rome's worst military defeats ever. It set the stage for centuries of warfare between Rome and her greatest imperial rival, Parthia/Persia. Indeed, despite her awesome military capacity, Rome was never able to overcome the military threat from Persia.

Crassus' defeat and death provoked outrage in Rome and calls for military reprisals, but Rome was in no position militarily or politically to avenge the setback. The rivalry between Caesar and Pompey had hardened and, with the dissolution of the First Triumvirate, Rome trembled at the prospect of another civil war.

The Fall of the Republic

In 52 B.C. Caesar cemented his military reputation with a decisive victory over a coalition of Gauls led by the hero-warrior Vercingetorix. In 50 B.C., his five-year extended consulship expired, and the Senate ordered Caesar to disband his army and return to Rome. Caesar recognized that the time had come for decisive action. Compliance with the Senate mandate would mean the end of his political career, given the hostility of most of his senatorial colleagues, Pompey in particular. He chose instead, to the everlasting regret of history, to risk all for the sake of his ambition and cast aside forever the brittle husk of the old republic. On January 10, 49 B.C., Caesar crossed the Rubicon River, which marked the Italian frontier, with his Tenth Legion, reputedly uttering the phrase that has become synonymous with irreversible, all-or-nothing decisions: "Alea jacta est" ("The die is cast").

With his battle-hardened veterans, Caesar stormed southwards, prompting Pompey, Cato, and others of the so-called "Optimates" (the party opposed to Caesar) to flee Rome. Perhaps Pompey wanted to spare the Eternal City the bloodbaths it had seen during the wars between Marius and Sulla, or perhaps Caesar's swiftness and resolution dismayed him, but Pompey the invincible found himself needing to regroup to prepare to meet Caesar's challenge. Caesar may have sought reconciliation with his rival, but the mask was now off, and Pompey wasn't having any. Their forces collided first at Dyrrachium in Greece, where Pompey's experience and able generalship carried the day in July, 48 B.C.

At this point, Pompey was seized with reluctance to prosecute the war further, distressed at the prospect of shedding more Roman blood. Cato the Younger, according to Plutarch, wept bitter tears at the sight of thousands of dead Romans on the battlefield after Dyrrachium. But most of Pompey's other associates urged him to pursue Caesar, to finish him off while his forces were reeling. Tormented by premonitions of disaster, Pompey bowed to the demands of his men and led them to the place where all would be hazarded, Pharsalus in northern Greece.

Only about a month had elapsed since Dyrrachium, and Pompey's forces greatly outnumbered those of his determined adversary. Yet Julius Caesar's army carried the day, routing Pompey's 45,000-man force and capturing all of his tents and equipment. Caesar, as was his trademark, was magnanimous with captured enemy leaders. He pardoned them all, judging that he would do better to win allies by showing mercy.

Pompey, Cato, and a number of others eluded capture, however. Pompey set sail, along with his wife and a substantial entourage, hoping to reach Africa and regroup. Reaching the coast of Egypt, Pompey was lured onto the beach by emissaries of the Egyptian monarch Ptolemy, who had decided to have Pompey murdered to ingratiate himself with Caesar. As his horrified wife and friends watched from the boat, the treacherous Egyptians cut down Pompey on the beach.

Caesar, pursuing Pompey to Egypt, appeared to be genuinely upset at the latter's assassination, since it denied him yet another opportunity to put his self-serving victor's magnanimity on display. As Plutarch noted, without a trace of irony, "in his letter to his friends at Rome, [Caesar] told them that the greatest and most signal pleasure his victory had given him was to be able continually to save the lives of fellow-citizens who had

A monarch uncrowned: Caesar, understanding the distasteful symbolism of a coronation, publicly refused a crown that Mark Antony tried to give him. It was probably a cynical publicity stunt, since Caesar had made himself a monarch in everything but name.

fought against him." In Egypt, Caesar supported Cleopatra in a civil war that had lately broken out and installed her as ruler. He also had an affair with Cleopatra that produced his only known son.

After a brief interlude in Asia Minor, where he defeated the latest upstart king of Pontus, Pharnaces II, the son of Mithridates, Caesar returned to Africa to deal with the remnants of the forces representing Pompey and the Senate. Another characteristically decisive victory followed, which saw most of the remaining opposition leadership killed. Cato the Younger, who was also in Africa, was informed of the defeat and of Caesar's great anxiousness to capture him as prelude to one of his famous reconciliations. But Cato, idealist, courageous patriot, and unshakable partisan of the old republic, wanted no part of the new order that Caesar was creating. Seeing that the republic was lost beyond recovery, he denied Caesar any personal triumph in the only way he knew how — by committing suicide.

Pompey's sons escaped to Spain, where they decided to make a last stand against Julius Caesar. Now in his fourth term as consul, Caesar hurried to Spain, the last of Rome's dominions to defy his rule, and destroyed the last opposing army at the Battle of Munda in 45 B.C., in which more than 30,000 Romans perished. Caesar himself, now in his fifties, is said to have led his reluctant men in an all-out charge. This time, however, he may have pushed his luck too far, for in the total victory at Munda he wiped out all the remaining family and confederates of Pompey, save only one son who escaped the carnage. This, Plutarch tells us, displeased large numbers of Romans who still held Pompey in very high esteem. Not only that, Caesar arrogantly celebrated this victory with a colossal triumph in Rome, which stirred up even more antagonism.

Nevertheless, he managed to get himself appointed dictator for life and elected to a 10-year term as consul. He shrewdly curried favor with the masses by publicly repudiating calls for him to be crowned king. In one incident — probably staged — his political ally and fellow consul Marcus Antonius (Mark Antony) attempted to crown him with a diadem during a major religious festival, but Caesar ostentatiously declined the honor, to the delight of onlookers. As Appian noted somberly, "the people hoped that [Caesar] would also give them back democracy, just as Sulla had done, who had achieved a position of equal power. However, they were disappointed in this."

According to Appian, Caesar's person was made inviolate, and he began conducting business from a throne of ivory and gold. Temples were dedicated to him, and the priests and priestesses were instructed to offer public prayers on his behalf. Magistrates were placed under oath not to oppose any of Caesar's decisions. Even a month of the Roman calendar, Quintus, was renamed Julius (July) in his honor.

Caesar used his dictatorial powers to redistribute wealth and land. He began planning grandiose public works and even reformed the Roman calendar. His most ambitious dream was a grand military campaign into Parthia and Scythia, and thence north and west into Germania, to bring under Roman dominion all of the nations to the north and east that still defied Roman arms.

Death of a Dictator

The recently expired republic, however, still had its champions. Cicero maintained a low profile, opting to play the survivor rather than the martyr. Other senators, however, led by Marcus Junius Brutus and Gaius Cassius Longinus, were dismayed at the Caesarian dictatorship. Brutus and Cassius had both been pardoned by Caesar after the defeat of Pompey, and young Brutus was even alleged by some to have been Caesar's illegitimate son. Brutus, Cassius, and their senatorial confederates now decided that only drastic action could restore the republic. They formed a conspiracy to assassinate Julius Caesar.

The date chosen for the assassination was March 15 in 44 B.C. According to tradition, Caesar had ample warning of the plot against him. His associates warned him that trouble was brewing, and a soothsayer advised him to beware of the Ides of March, as the Romans referred to that fateful day. On the eve before his assassination, his wife Calpurnia dreamt that he had

81

been murdered and begged him to stay at home the next day.

Yet in spite of all these portents, Caesar made his way to the Forum the next day. Plutarch records that he met the soothsayer along the way and told him jestingly, "The Ides of March are come;" to which the soothsayer, unruffled, replied, "Yes, they are come, but they are not past."

On that day, the Senate had chosen to meet in a building where a great statue of Pompey stood. It was at the very foot of this statue, as Caesar was surrounded by a knot of senators, that the assassins, bearing daggers concealed under their togas, made their move. As soon as he realized what was happening, Caesar fought ferociously against his assailants, but soon sank to his knees. Seeing Brutus among the assassins, he is supposed to have said, "Even you, my child?" before succumbing to more than 20 knife wounds.

After the assassination, the senators fled in confusion, and Rome descended into turmoil. The man who had dealt the republic its death blow was dead in his turn, but contrary to the expectations of his assassins, few Romans rallied now to the cause of the republic. Instead, the masses mourned the passing of a charismatic leader who had kept them entertained and who had never hesitated to raid the public treasury on their behalf. Instead of liberty, Rome now craved peace, luxury, and security. But with the permanent rise of Caesarism, Rome lost not only her liberty but also her peace and security. Her opulence and fearsome military machine guaranteed yet a few generations of imperial dominance, but for Rome's unhappy citizens, the years to come would bring a nightmarish pageant of bloodshed and oppression that in the end would undo the civilizing work of centuries and bring to a close the first flowering of Western civilization.

Thus ever to tyrants: Caesar's assassins wanted to restore the republic by killing a usurper, but only made matters worse. Many Romans loved Caesar for his generosity with public monies and for his military prowess, and had lost interest in self-government.

CHAPTER 8

FROM REPUBLIC TO EMPIRE

The assassins of Julius Caesar hoped to restore the Roman Republic, but they instead set in motion events that encouraged the rise and triumph of despots worse than Caesar.

The assassination of Julius Caesar, instead of solving Rome's problems, had made them worse. Brutus, Cassius, and the

Death of Cicero: Betrayed by Octavian and proscribed by the bloodthirsty Mark Antony, Cicero was tracked down by government assassins at a remote villa, where he resignedly offered his neck to the sword.

85

other assassins ran through the streets of Rome with blood on their hands and togas, proclaiming liberty and the death of the tyrant. They were greeted for the most part by sullen stares, while the remainder of the Roman government fled the Forum in confusion, expecting perhaps that this latest blow to Rome could only lead to more pogroms. Before long, Brutus and Cassius realized that, rather than ridding Rome of a detested tyrant, they had made a martyr out of a popular despot.

Two men who watched events unfold with opportunistic glee were Mark Antony, Caesar's junior consular partner, and Octavian, Caesar's adopted son (and the son of Caesar's niece), who was barely 20 years of age. Mark Antony feigned solidarity with the assassins until the day of Caesar's funeral. When he eulogized Caesar, he took advantage of the solemn occasion to heap imprecations on Caesar's assassins and displayed Caesar's bloody, slashed toga to the onlookers. The crowd, enraged at the sight, surged into the streets to hunt down and kill Caesar's murderers. They tore to pieces an innocent bystander who happened to have the same name as one of the assassins, prompting Brutus, Cassius, and the rest to flee Rome.

While Cassius and Brutus escaped to Greece to try to raise armies of their own, Antony set about consolidating power for himself. He soon found his popularity on the wane, thanks in large measure to Cicero. The tireless statesman delivered to the Senate and the Assemblies a total of 14 passionate speeches denouncing Antony and his tyrannical ambitions, calling them — only half in jest — his Philippics, after the Greek orator Demosthenes' celebrated denunciations of Philip of Macedon. At the same time, Octavian, having returned to Rome, became Antony's great rival. He adopted for himself the title of Caesar and soon garnered enough factional support to force Antony temporarily to withdraw from the city.

But Octavian in his turn quickly learned what his adopted father had understood: the road to absolute power would be more secure if reinforced by willing allies. With a political precocity that belied his extreme youth, Octavian sent emissaries both to Antony and to a third man, Lepidus, a former consul and

Funeral of a dictator: Mark Antony exploited Caesar's funeral to stir up the Roman masses against Caesar's assassins. The mob burned the houses of Cassius and Brutus, but the two men escaped to make a final attempt to rescue the republic.

staunch ally of both Julius Caesar and Antony, proposing reconciliation. Antony and Lepidus both seized the olive branch and with Octavian formed, in 43 B.C., the unholy alliance known as the Second Triumvirate.

The Proscriptions

The first act of the triumvirs was to draw up a list of political enemies to be eliminated. This process required a certain amount of cynical give and take; Cicero, for example, had been a supporter of Octavian against Antony, but the latter now insisted on Cicero's death. According to Plutarch's version of events, "They [the triumvirs] met secretly and by themselves, for three days near the town of Bononia.... Caesar [i.e., Octavian] contended earnestly for Cicero the first two days; but on the third day he yielded, and gave him up. The terms of their mutual concessions were these: that Caesar should desert Cicero, Lepidus his brother Paulus, and Antony, Lucius Caesar, his uncle by his mother's side. Thus they let their anger and fury take from them the sense of humanity, and demonstrated that no beast is more savage than man when possessed with power answerable to his rage."

The assassins of the new Triumvirate now fanned out across Roman territory to eliminate the hundreds of Romans on the proscription lists. They tracked Cicero down at a remote villa by the sea, where, weary of flight, the aged statesman offered his neck willingly. His head and hands were taken back to Rome and delivered to a jubilant Antony, who ordered them fastened up over the rostra in the Senate, "a sight," Plutarch tells us, "which the Roman people shuddered to behold, and they believed they saw there, not the face of Cicero, but the image of Antony's own soul."

Last Stand at Philippi

Brutus and Cassius, hearing of the proscriptions and the death of Cicero, were hardened in their determination to hazard all for Old Rome. They had enjoyed considerable success in winning over or conquering portions of Greece, and their combined

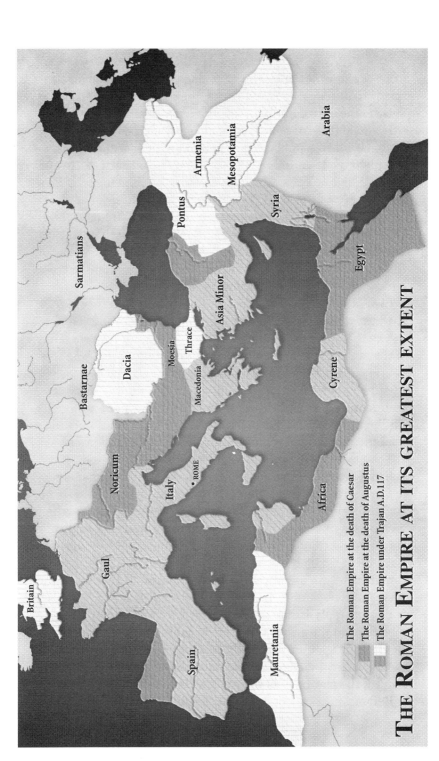

The Roman Empire at the death of Caesar
The Roman Empire at the death of Augustus
The Roman Empire under Trajan A.D.117

THE ROMAN EMPIRE AT ITS GREATEST EXTENT

Britain

Gaul

Spain

Noricum

Italy

• ROME

Mauretania

Africa

Bastarnae

Dacia

Moesia

Thrace

Macedonia

Sarmatians

Cyrene

Asia Minor

Pontus

Armenia

Mesopotamia

Syria

Egypt

Arabia

army was one of the largest that Rome had ever fielded. Having won Macedonia to their cause, they assembled their forces outside the city of Philippi, the provincial capital.

It is said that Marcus Brutus, along with Cassius, the leader of Rome's last republican army, had an extraordinary vision one night while encamped with his army in Asia Minor. He and Cassius had raised a vast military force to challenge the Second Triumvirate of Mark Antony, Octavian, and Lepidus, a sort of military junta assembled after the death of Julius Caesar. Brutus, sometimes called "the last Roman," knew that the time was fast approaching for a climactic battle with the forces of the Second Triumvirate, and was making preparations to cross back into Greece for the final confrontation.

Brutus was alone in his tent reading by lamplight, long after the rest of his men had gone to sleep. Suddenly he became aware that he was not alone and, looking toward the entrance of the tent, saw, in Plutarch's words, "a terrible and strange appearance" standing beside his bed. Brutus, undismayed, asked the apparition what it was and why it had come. "I am your evil genius, Brutus," the figure replied. "You shall see me at Philippi." Brutus stared at the dark figure with all the courage he could muster and replied evenly, "Then I shall see you."

The next day he told his friend and associate Cassius of the vision. Cassius reassured him, saying that the mind had limitless capacities for inventing such things and that there were no such things as supernatural beings. He added with more than a little irony, "I confess I wish that there were such beings, that we might not rely upon our arms only, and our horses and our navy, all of which are so numerous and powerful, but might be confident of the assistance of the gods also, in this our most sacred and honorable attempt."

Brutus' reply is not recorded. But with the Roman government now in the grip of tyrants, the old republic in tatters, and Rome embroiled in yet another titanic civil war, Brutus and many other trembling citizens must have wondered whether, indeed, the powers of heaven had abandoned them.

Before long, the combined armies of Octavian and Antony

made their appearance. On the morning of battle, October 27, 42 B.C., Brutus and Cassius conferred for what would be the last time. Cassius asked Brutus what he resolved to do if things went ill for them. "If Providence," Brutus replied, "shall not dispose what we now undertake according to our wishes, I resolve to put no further hopes or warlike preparations to the proof, but will die contented with my fortune. For I have already given up my life for my country on the Ides of March; and have lived since then a second life for her sake, with liberty and honor."

In the battle that followed, many thousands were hewn down on both sides. Octavian retired prudently from the field, which saved the young Caesar's life, since Brutus' republican forces fought their way to the enemy camp and pillaged it, setting to flight or killing large numbers of Octavian's troops. But on the other wing of the battle, Antony's men prevailed and sacked the camp of the republican forces. Thinking all was lost, Cassius, ever the pessimist, committed suicide. Brutus withdrew his forces from the battlefield to defend his camp, and the battle ended inconclusively. Eight thousand of the republican army lay dead on the battlefield and roughly twice that number from the forces of the Triumvirate.

The two armies regrouped and prepared for a second engagement. Brutus' navy, in the meantime, engaged that of Octavian and wiped it out, prompting Octavian to renew hostilities before Brutus could learn of his good fortune. On the evening of November 16, the dark apparition reputedly appeared to Brutus again, but vanished without saying a word. And on the following day, his forces met with disaster.

The battle was comparatively brief. The forces of the Triumvirate smashed through the republican lines. Marcus, the son of Cato the Younger, died a hero. Refusing to flee, he shouted his father's name over and over as enemy troops closed in about him, leaving many of them dead on the field before finally succumbing. Another of Brutus' men, Lucilius, pretended to be Brutus and allowed himself to be captured by Antony's forces, buying time for Brutus himself to escape. But Brutus, seeing the ruin of everything that he had lived and fought for, fell upon his sword.

91

Contest for Empire

With the final defeat of the republican forces, all that remained for the rival members of the Triumvirate was a battle for the prize of absolute power. Lepidus managed to avoid all-out war with Octavian and Antony, content with gradual diminution of his role until finally being removed from power in 36 B.C. Antony and Octavian, however, rekindled their earlier dispute. It soon became apparent that the Roman Empire was not large enough for both of them.

The first rift occurred in 41 B.C., with a revolt against Octavian led by Fulvia, Antony's wife. Octavian quashed the revolt the following year, and Fulvia died in exile. Octavian and Antony patched things up temporarily with Antony's marriage to Octavia, Octavian's half-sister.

Antony's affair with Queen Cleopatra of Egypt led to a permanent and irreconcilable break between the two triumvirs, Octavian accusing Antony of repudiating his Roman birthright to pursue an adulterous liaison with the Egyptian queen, and Antony accusing Octavian of usurping power that rightfully

Battle of Actium: Regarded as one of the most important naval battles in history, Actium — which ended with the fiery destruction of Antony's fleet — decided nothing except which of two tyrants would inherit the imperial spoils.

belonged to Ptolemy Caesar, also known as Caesarion, the illegitimate son of Caesar and Cleopatra. Tensions simmered for a number of years before open civil war again ignited in 31 B.C. The climactic engagement took place in the gulf of Actium on September 2, in which the navies of Antony and Cleopatra squared off against Octavian's navy in the greatest sea battle until Lepanto, 16 centuries later. In the midst of the battle, Cleopatra fled in her ship, and Antony forsook the battle to pursue her. The forces of Octavian finally wiped out Antony's navy by setting the fleet on fire, incinerating thousands of men.

With the final defeat of Antony and Cleopatra, who fled to Egypt and soon committed suicide, the decade-long struggle for uncontested dominion was at an end. Yet still the young Caesar wavered, according to historian Cassius Dio, as to whether to forge ahead as Rome's sole ruler or to attempt to restore republican government. We can only speculate as to Octavian's sincerity, but one of his advisers, Agrippa, counseled him to eschew monarchy. "I do not see what reason could possibly persuade you to desire to become sole ruler," he told the young autocrat. "Such a regime is difficult to impose upon democracies in general, and would be far more difficult still for you yourself to operate. Surely you can see how the city of Rome and its affairs are even now in a state of turmoil. It is difficult in the first place to make yourself master of the mass of our citizens who have lived for so many years in freedom, and secondly it is difficult, when we are surrounded by so many enemies, to reduce once more to slavery the allies and the subject nations, bearing in mind that some have been democratically governed for generations, and others we ourselves have set free." Agrippa pointed out the many advantages of free states over tyrannies and recommended that Octavian set the affairs of the state in order and then lay aside the scepter:

> Act wisely, while you have the opportunity, and entrust to the people the control of the army, the provinces, the offices of state and the public funds. If you do this now and of your own accord, you will be at once the most famous of men and

Cleopatra on her ship: The Egyptian queen, who had borne Julius Caesar's illegitimate son, later had a famous affair with Mark Antony. In the heat of battle at Actium, however, she turned tail and sailed away, contributing to Antony's catastrophic defeat.

the most secure.... It would be an immensely hard task to bring this city, which has known democratic government for so many years, and which rules an empire of such a size, to a state of slavery.... The state of monarchy is such that even virtuous men cannot possibly redeem it.

Agrippa reminded the sovereign that certain men, like Sulla, had been able to lay aside supreme authority and retire, and recommended that Octavian do the same.

Octavian's other adviser, Maecenas, was of the opposite opinion. He urged Octavian to accept the reality of empire and to indulge no further vain hopes that the republic could ever be reconstituted. "So long as our numbers were not large and we did not differ in any important respects from our neighbors," he pointed out, "our system of government worked well, and we brought almost the whole of Italy under our rule. But ever since we ventured beyond our native soil, crossed the water, set foot on many islands and many continents, and filled the whole sea and the whole earth with our name and power, we have experienced nothing but ill fortune. At first it was only at home and within our own walls that we split into factions and quarreled with one another, but later we introduced this sickness even into the army. For this reason our city, like a great merchant vessel, manned with a crew of every race but lacking a pilot, has now for many generations continued to roll and plunge as it drifted here and there in a heavy sea.... Do not, then, allow her to be waterlogged. And do not let her be smashed to pieces on a reef, for her timbers are rotten and she will not be able to hold out much longer." Republican government was clearly inadequate to the demands of a far-flung, multi-ethnic empire and the vast military that held it together, but rather than renounce imperial dominion, Maecenas preferred to renounce liberty.

After his counselors finished, Octavian, who had now adopted the title Caesar Augustus, thanked them both for their sincerity and openness. Unsurprisingly it was, according to Dio, "the advice of Maecenas that he was inclined to accept."

The Roman people and the Senate, exhausted by decades of

warfare and domestic turmoil, and bereft of the leadership of a Cicero or a Brutus, wearily resigned themselves to the loss of their republic. The Senate and various magistracies — the forms of republicanism — were preserved by Augustus, but shorn of meaningful power. The senators, the emperor made clear, were now his subordinates. He purged the Senate of refractory elements by compelling hundreds of senators to resign without open reprisals. He also forbade the remaining senators from ever traveling outside of Italy, a law that remained in force in Rome ever after.

Augustus made much fanfare out of closing, in 29 B.C., the doors of the temple of Janus. Roman custom for centuries had decreed that the doors remain open in time of war and be closed only during peace. For many generations, the doors had been kept open, in acknowledgement of the endless warfare that had afflicted Rome since her earliest forays into imperialism. Imperial Rome was now at peace, for the time being. But it was a peace dearly bought, as succeeding generations would discover. Augustus himself was the most benign emperor Rome was to see for a century and a half, but his immediate successors, beginning with Tiberius and continuing with a hundred-year parade of brutal monsters, were soon to teach Rome — and the entire Western world — the true price of empire.

CHAPTER 9

ROME'S DARK NIGHT OF TYRANNY

When the republic fell, Rome entered the dark decline of empire. Only after centuries of misery under predominantly tyrannical emperors did Rome finally meet its end.

In the fourth century of our era, the Danube River marked the northern frontier of the Roman Empire. To the north and east

Rome prostrate: Alaric the Goth surveys Rome prior to entering and sacking the city. Alaric, a Christian, was benign compared to later conquerors, like Attila and Genseric, who dismembered the empire.

of the Danube, fierce Germanic and Scythian tribes roamed to the edges of the known world. Beyond them — according to the uncertain traditions of the ancients — lay a savage, frozen wilderness populated by the likes of the Geloni, who dressed in the skins of their slain enemies, and the Melanchlaenae, who fed on human flesh.

Immediately to the north of the eastern Danube were vast settlements of Goths, who by the mid-370s found themselves threatened by invading Huns and

Alans from the east. To escape the ravaging barbarians from the hinterlands, the Goths fled en masse to the banks of the Danube and sent envoys to the Roman emperor Valens, begging for permission to cross into Roman territory to escape the marauding hordes, and to settle in the province of Thrace. Valens, persuaded of the need for a mercenary and labor force to fortify and protect the northern boundaries of the empire, and anxious to expand his tax base, made one of the most fateful decisions in all of history: he opened the borders of the empire and invited the Goths to immigrate to Roman territory.

With the help of boats furnished by the Romans, the Goths poured across the Danube into Roman territory — "like lava from Etna," in the words of Roman historian Ammianus Marcellinus — and set up encampments in Thrace. The occupying population was estimated by Edward Gibbon to have numbered at least 200,000 fighting men and up to a million total immigrants. The Romans immediately took advantage of the situation by bartering food and other necessaries (including, supposedly, spoiled dog meat) to the desperate Goths, in exchange for slaves. The Goths resented such treatment and soon rebelled against the Roman authorities. Before too many months, the Goths, led by their crafty general, Fritigern, were pillaging and laying waste to cities all across Thrace.

Disaster at Hadrianople

After several bloody and indecisive battles, the Roman emperor Valens himself decided to intervene. He marched north at the head of an enormous army that represented much of the military might of Rome and encountered the Gothic army — which was now allied to and strengthened by Alan and Hun auxiliaries — outside the city of Hadrianople. Hadrianople, the "city of Hadrian," was named for the emperor best remembered for the fortifications he built on another Roman frontier, the boundary between Roman and Celtic Britain, known as "Hadrian's Wall." On August 9, 378 A.D., the plains outside the city of Hadrian witnessed the battle that brought the Roman Empire to her knees.

Valens and his forces advanced confidently against the howling barbarian host, only to be outflanked and outfought by the furious Goths, who had cleverly postponed the engagement until the heat of the day, when the Romans were weakened and dehydrated. Crushed together by the furious onslaught, the Romans, unable to maneuver or even use their swords and javelins, were slaughtered like cattle. By the end of that terrible day, the flower of the Roman military had been cut down, including 35 tribunes, many distinguished generals, and Valens himself, whose body was never recovered. With them fell somewhere between 50,000 and 100,000 Roman soldiers, or up to 80 percent of the entire existing Roman military force.

Not since Cannae in the Second Punic War had Rome suffered such a disaster. But unlike Cannae, which became a rallying point for republican Rome, Hadrianople shattered the empire beyond repair. Over the next few decades, the empire was swept away by successive invasions of barbarians eager to take advantage of Rome's undefended borders.

Within 30 years of the disaster in Thrace, Alaric and his Gothic horde were besieging the Eternal City. By 429 A.D., the Vandals were pouring into Roman North Africa, and in 455 they sacked Rome itself. Attila and his Huns, most formidable of all, overran much of Greece, Italy, and Gaul in the early decades of the fifth century, leaving desolation in their wake. Well could Romans, by the mid-fifth century, lament the fateful decision of a weak and foolish emperor, and what Ammianus mournfully called the "tumultuous eagerness of those who urged on the proceedings [that] led to the destruction of the Roman world."

The disaster at Hadrianople was, however, a symptom, not a cause, of Roman imperial decline. In historical hindsight, the longevity of the Roman Empire was extraordinary, given the centuries of almost unrelenting tyranny, warfare, economic decay, and even natural disasters that ravaged the once-proud Roman dominions. That the weary denizens of the empire could have endured so many generations of grinding tyranny is a testimony to human endurance. But more than a few may have felt a sense of relief at the collapse of their imperial oppressors.

The Roman Empire proper had begun with Octavian, better known as Caesar Augustus, who, after Actium, had a subsequent reign of more than 40 years of comparative tranquility, in spite of atrocities committed by certain of his imperial subordinates, like the Judean tetrarch Herod. But with the death of Augustus in 14 A.D., a new type of monarch assumed the scepter in Rome, embodied in Augustus' adopted son Tiberius.

Darkness Falls

Tiberius, like nearly all of his imperial successors, was a monster. "If we were to draw a picture of his life," wrote the Abbé Millot, a historian held in high esteem by the American Founding Fathers, "we might say that he knew what was good, and often commanded it, but the general tenor of his conduct was to do evil with cool deliberate malevolence." One of Tiberius' first acts in office was to order the assassination of Agrippa, the son of Augustus' most famous adviser of the same name. He was also accused of ordering the murder of Germanicus, a Roman military leader of great integrity who had successfully put down a sedition in the military aiming to set him up as emperor in Tiberius' stead. But instead of the emperor's gratitude, Germanicus' popularity with the Roman people earned him only Tiberius' bitter envy.

Tiberius set up a massive network of informers, and passed laws making writings or utterances critical of his regime high treason, and punishable by death. If Julius Caesar and Octavian had transformed the Roman Republic into a military dictatorship, Tiberius now changed it into a police state.

In addition to his political cruelty, Tiberius, if the frank testimony of Suetonius is to be believed, was a depraved monster in his private life. A recitation of the details of Tiberius' private life would appall and sicken the reader; it is enough to record that Tiberius was an enthusiastic and insatiable practitioner of every base sexual depravity known, and even kept vast numbers of captive children to gratify his twisted whims.

Tiberius, like most of Rome's emperors, met a violent end. Having fallen severely ill, he was suffocated by certain of his at-

Rogues' gallery: Of these first-century Roman leaders, only Germanicus and Augustus were not total monsters. Tiberius, Caligula, and Nero in particular were among the most bestial princes history has ever produced.

tendants after partly recovering from a bout of illness that had been expected to claim his evil life. He was succeeded by Gaius Germanicus, also known as Caligula, a man whose perversions and despotic behavior have always taxed the credulity of modern historians. Caligula carried on incestuous relationships with his three sisters. He had numerous homosexual partners and forced adulterous liaisons with many of Rome's most illustrious women.

Caligula took full advantage of the police-state apparatus founded by his predecessor to unleash a reign of terror unsurpassed (though often matched) in imperial Roman history. A brief excerpt from Suetonius' lengthy and horrifying description of Caligula's reign will give the reader an idea of Rome under Caligula's administration:

> Gaius made parents attend their sons' executions, and when one father excused himself on the ground of ill health, provided a litter for him.... A knight, on the point of being thrown to the wild beasts, shouted that he was innocent; Gaius brought him back, removed his tongue, and then ordered the sentence to be carried out.... The method of execution he preferred was to inflict numerous small wounds; and his familiar order: "Make him feel that he is dying!" soon became proverbial.

"Let them hate me, so long as they fear me," Caligula is alleged to have often said. On one well-known occasion, Caligula, angry at crowds cheering a team he opposed, publicly wished that all Romans had but one neck to sever. He terrorized Romans of every social class, delighting in mass executions of senators and in having prisoners tortured in his presence during mealtime. His erratic behavior suggests what Suetonius and others have concluded, that Caligula was clinically insane. Caligula was assassinated after terrorizing Rome for nearly four years.

He was succeeded by Claudius, another monster, somewhat less bloodthirsty, but fickle and depraved nonetheless. Claudius appears to have been of subnormal intelligence, which made him susceptible to manipulation by amoral power-mongers like his appalling wife Messalina.

Dean of Depravity

Claudius, who was finally poisoned by assassins, was followed by another bestial personage whose name, like that of Adolf Hitler, has become virtually synonymous with wanton dictatorial cruelty: Nero. This new emperor was a man of many gifts. He had an aptitude for the arts and was an accomplished musician. He was a man of considerable charisma and had a photographic memory for names and faces. His reign started promisingly; he pledged to restore the practices of civilized rule that had characterized the Augustan period, and he lowered taxes dramatically. However, he soon began spending extravagant sums on lavish games and other public entertainment extravaganzas.

As a portent of further ill to come, his penchant for monstrous personal vices gradually gained the upper hand. All of the perversions of his predecessors were Nero's stock in trade. Suetonius accuses him of committing frequent incest with his mother Agrippina, of raping a vestal virgin, and of attempting to convert one of his young male consorts into a woman by mutilating him and forcing him to undergo a wedding in bridal attire. And these, if Suetonius is given credibility, were among his milder vices.

His bloodlust turned Rome into a horror show for 14 awful years. In addition to murdering many members of his own family, including his mother and aunt, Nero continued the reign of terror of his predecessors in emphatic style. The best-known episode in his misbegotten rule, the great conflagration that destroyed Rome, was quite possibly his own doing, although the historical evidence for that is inconclusive. What seems beyond dispute was that he reveled in the destruction and played his lyre as the Eternal City went up in flames.

Persecutions and Power Factions

In the aftermath, Nero encouraged the belief that members of a new religion, Christians, were to blame, and launched the most horrific large-scale persecutions that Christianity had yet seen. In the words of Tacitus, "an immense multitude [of Christians] was convicted, not so much of the crime of firing the city, as of hatred against mankind. Mockery of every sort was added to their deaths. Covered with the skins of wild beasts, they were torn by dogs and perished, or were nailed to the crosses, or were doomed to the flames and burnt, to serve as a nightly illumination, when daylight had expired."

Nero's behavior finally brought about armed revolt, led by Galba, who marched on Rome in 68 A.D. Nero committed suicide as Galba's forces closed in. Rome for the next several years was the scene of unending slaughter and civil war, as three more bloodthirsty tyrants — Galba, Otho, and Vitellius — succeeded to the purple by violent overthrow. Tacitus gives vivid descriptions of Rome ravaged by fire and the sword again and again, and of thousands of terrified citizens cut down by successive power factions. Suetonius, never one to mince words, complements Tacitus' account with his usual revolting personal portraits of these men.

It was during this period that the Roman military acquired a habit it was seldom to relinquish for the remainder of the empire: proclaiming emperors solely on the authority and whim of the soldiers. Unlike later European monarchies, imperial Rome (as well as its successor regime in the east, Byzantium) never developed a system of orderly succession, with the result that almost all emperors were enthroned by armed revolt culminating in the murder of their predecessor and of any potential rivals.

If the Christians had endured unspeakable persecution under Nero, it was the turn of the Jews to do the same under Vespasian and Titus, the latter of whom finally destroyed Jerusalem in a horrific campaign that resulted in the destruction of the temple and the slaughter of hundreds of thousands of Jews.

By the end of the first century A.D., Rome and her dominions had endured several generations of horror and bloodshed on a scale and duration never before seen in human history. Even the architectural remnants of republican Rome had been swept

Mass martyrdom: The emperor Nero publicly blamed Christians for the great fire that destroyed Rome in 64 A.D. — a fire he may have set himself. At his orders, thousands of Christians were burned alive all across the city.

away by the fires that had scoured the city, and every last vestige of republican virtue and manners had been eradicated. The Senate still existed in name, and would persist as a feeble institution for several centuries, but old Rome had been consumed in the holocaust of empire.

Beginning with the emperor Nerva and continuing with Trajan, Hadrian, Antoninus, and Marcus Aurelius, imperial Rome from the late first century until the death of Marcus Aurelius in 180 A.D. enjoyed a brief sunlit interlude that saw the flowering of Christianity and the production of many great works of literature, including the writings of Plutarch and Tacitus. It was this period that Gibbon chose as his point of departure in his famous *History of the Decline and Fall of the Roman Empire* — a misleading starting point to support his mistaken premise that the early empire represented the pinnacle of Roman achievement. Calling the empire "the most civilized portion of mankind," Gibbon went on to extol Rome's "disciplined valor," "peaceful inhabitants," "free constitution," and "gentle, but powerful, influence of laws and manners." However, Rome during this comparatively placid interval was still a decrepit civilization of unending foreign wars and conquests, of palace intrigue, and of the debased morals that had incubated the likes of Caligula and Nero. The virtues of Nerva, Trajan, Hadrian, and the two Antonines appear magnified by the faults of their predecessors. But with the death of Marcus Aurelius, Rome's lucky streak ended.

Empire's End

Marcus Aurelius was succeeded by his son Commodus, another bestial ruler cast from the same mold as Nero, with the same vices and insatiable appetite for cruelty. He was eventually strangled by a gladiator in the employ of a palace conspiracy.

And so it went. For the next several hundred years, the Roman Empire was strained to the breaking point by civil wars, foreign adventures, heavy taxation, and constant political turmoil. Emperor succeeded emperor, usually by violence. For each tolerable ruler — a Diocletian, Pertinax, Constantine, or Julian

Rome vandalized: Led by the fearsome Genseric, the Vandals, a Germanic tribe that had already wrested Iberia and North Africa from the Roman Empire, sacked and burned Rome itself in 455 A.D. After centuries of impregnability, Rome was now experiencing the same horrors her legions had so often inflicted on others.

— there were a dozen monsters, such as Caracalla, Elagabalus, Maximin, Valens, and others far too numerous to merit mention. Most of them slashed their way to the top, only to be deposed in bloody coups within weeks or months of accession to the purple. And even the best were deeply flawed or committed unpardonable atrocities.

Constantine the Great, despite establishing Christianity as the official religion of Rome, was capable of remarkable acts of cruelty, which included having his own wife and son put to death. Julian, nicknamed "the Apostate," was a brilliant and able leader, but chose to persecute Christians and to wage unprovoked war on the Persian Empire, where he died of battle wounds during the retreat from Ctesiphon, the Persian capital. Pertinax, who followed Commodus, seems to have been a genuinely virtuous man. He attempted to restore Senate authority, transferred all his personal property to his wife and son to avoid the reproach of personal enrichment, and overturned the unjust decrees of his predecessor. Unfortunately, this decent man was murdered by his own Praetorian guards after less than three months as emperor. Imperial Rome was beyond repair and no longer suited to virtuous leadership.

Diocletian, who reigned for 20 years, divided the empire for the first time, a division that became permanent in the midfourth century in the time of Valentinian I and Valens. At about this same time, in July 365 A.D., the Roman world was literally shaken by an unprecedented catastrophe. An immense earthquake struck the greater part of the Mediterranean basin and was followed by gigantic tsunamis that wiped out much of coastal Sicily, Dalmatia, Greece, and Egypt. The great city of Alexandria was nearly destroyed, losing 50,000 inhabitants. This event filled the Roman world, pagans and Christians alike, with consternation, as the very powers of nature now seemed to be unleashed against the dying Roman world. Thirteen years later came the calamitous battle of Hadrianople, the event that traditionally marks the beginning of the Dark Ages.

After Hadrianople, predatory barbarian tribes were quick to pounce on the enfeebled Roman world, and by the late fifth century, the last remnant of the Western Roman Empire was conquered by the Goths and other tribes. Many of the Germanic tribes, most conspicuously the Goths, did possess a certain rustic virtue, enhanced by their Arian Christian beliefs. Gothic rulers of former Roman dominions, like Theodoric and Totila, were fairly just and humane rulers compared to the morally bankrupt Romans, and many former imperial citizens were happy to submit to these gentler masters. Meanwhile, the Eastern Empire lived on, with its capital at Constantinople and its distinctly Greek and Asiatic character, for another thousand years.

Thus did Rome die, more than 1,300 years after the founding of the city by Romulus and his band of followers. Following the historian Gibbon's description of Roman history, much has been made of the decline and fall of the empire, but the real story, which had concluded by the time of Christ, was the decline and fall of the republic. For the fall of empires is a foregone conclusion; they are always built on foundations of sand — despotism, militarism, expansionism, and welfarism — and soon exhaust themselves, or are dismembered by other powers. But the causes leading to the decline and fall of republics pose a vexing problem that man has not yet fully fathomed.

CHAPTER 10

LESSONS OF ROME

The rise and fall of the Roman Republic provides lessons that hint at flaws in modern political policies.

From a modern vantage point, Roman history instructs poignantly on both the genius of prudent government and the folly of empire. Imperial Rome was finally extinguished in the fifth century A.D., and though strands of her culture persisted — in the Venetian Republic, in the Byzantine Empire, and in Western Christendom, which preferred the Latin language over the vernacular for the next thousand years — the books were closed on the civilization of Cicero, Brutus, and even the Caesars. Because well-constituted states usually decline gradually rather

Remains to be seen: Millions of people have marveled at the ruins of the Roman Forum, which was once the setting for some of the greatest political dramas, and some of the most extraordinary leaders, in all of human history.

than suddenly, the lessons of Rome were centuries in the teaching — centuries that, to most Romans, made the loss of Roman liberty only vaguely noticeable.

The primary reason for Rome's fall was moral decline. Every Roman writer who chronicled the fall of the republic — Appian, Tacitus, Cassius Dio, Sallust, Cicero, and others — marveled at the evaporation of ancient virtue that preceded the loss of liberty. While republican Rome lacked many of the softer virtues of later Christian civilization, there can be no question that, in comparison with most contemporary pagan societies, Rome was a paragon of rectitude, resisting for centuries many of the debilitating vices and superstitions of the rest of the pagan world. Where the Greeks institutionalized homosexual behavior, sexual perversion was taboo in the Roman Republic. Where the Carthaginians practiced human sacrifice, including child sacrifice on a large scale, Rome generally refrained from such excesses. Where Persia, and Babylonia before her, submitted to an all-powerful priesthood who were superior in power to political rulers, Roman priests remained subordinate to magistrates of the republic.

Cultural Revolution

The end of the republic saw a revolution not only in political but in moral and even religious manners. By the first century B.C., sexual mores had been abandoned, and the former sanctity of marriage forgotten. Crime, once almost unknown in Rome, became rampant. In such an environment, Rome became an easy target for political conspiracies like that of Catiline, which exploited the criminal elements in Rome to carry out bribery, blackmail, and assassination.

More ominously still, the bucolic simplicity of authentic Roman religion was gradually contaminated by a monstrous cult from the east, the Persian mystery religion of Mithra that, by the late second century A.D., had permeated every level of Roman society. This cult was in fact a vast secret society consecrated to emperor-worship and to the amoral doctrine of radical dualism — the idea that good and evil are eternal, absolutely equivalent principles that must both be appeased. It was apparently introduced into Rome in the first century B.C. by the Cilician pirates and spread through the ranks of political officialdom and the military, claiming as adherents emperors like Commodus, Aurelian, Diocletian, and Julian.

Fortunately for Western civilization, Christianity eventually eclipsed Mithraism, breathing new life into decrepit imperial Rome. Rome's successor civilization in the East, Byzantium, was sustained for more than a thousand years by the Christian piety of her citizens and more capable rulers, despite ceaseless assaults by barbarian nations and an irremediably weak system of law and government.

Wages of War

Much of Rome's strength in her early years flowed from her martial virtues. Her citizen soldiers were fearless and superbly organized. The Roman genius for order soon led to innovations in military science that made the Roman legions a virtually invincible fighting force for centuries. But Rome's military successes engendered a love of conflict and conquest that hastened her undoing. For republican Rome was unwilling to interrupt her ceaseless warfare at the water's edge, and plunged into overseas empire building at the first challenge from abroad.

The Punic wars were followed by several generations of mostly craven conquest against much weaker foes in Iberia, Africa, and Asia Minor. Caesar's victories over the Gauls were mostly achieved by playing disunited tribes against one another, and further encouraged Rome to trust in her own invincibility. Yet when Rome was confronted with truly formidable foes, the results were sometimes calamitous. Such was the case with the Parthians at Carrhae and the Germans at Teutoberg, both of which resulted in the slaughter of entire legions.

In the imperial period, the sturdy Gothic nation, unimpressed by Rome's inflated opinion of herself, became Rome's most successful adversary. To the north, the Germans never succumbed to Roman arms, and to the east, the Persian empire of the Sassanids presented an impossible challenge. But Rome, once addicted to international warfare, never found the strength of will to lay down the sword. Her endless wars of conquest depleted her coffers (despite the plunders of war), decimated her population, made enemies far and wide — and created irresistible pressure for surrendering domestic liberties.

For Rome, her greatest civic strength had always been her unity. Until the late second century B.C., Rome had never seen bloodshed from civil unrest. The various disputes between the plebeians and patricians had always been resolved by negotiation and political reform. But beginning with the administrations of the Gracchi in the late second century B.C., Rome exploded into episodes of partisan violence. The following century saw a series of devastating civil wars that tore the republic apart and eased the way for the rise of military dictators like Caesar, Antony, and Octavian, who put an end to Roman liberties. From that time forward, Rome was never free from factional violence. Political assassinations and riots, unknown in the early centuries of the republic, became commonplace. Emperors were enthroned and deposed almost exclusively by military coups, often accompanied by dreadful purges and epic battles.

Constitutional Flaws

In matters of law, the Roman constitution, superior though it was to other contemporary political systems, contained a number of serious flaws that came to the fore as the republic disintegrated. For one thing, it provided for the appointment of dictators for six-month periods during times of acute crisis, an institution that furnished a pretext for military coups by the likes of Marius, Sulla, and Caesar. For another, the Roman constitution failed to give equal protection to all Roman citizens, institutionalizing the patrician aristocracy and ensuring that Rome would always have a ruling class.

While the Roman system of government recognized the need for checks and balances and for separating the powers of the state among various offices and magistracies, the Roman state did not enjoy the neat modern divisions of executive, legisla-

Factional strife: When Rome's military forces were turned against her own people, from the first century B.C. onwards, the resulting purges often decimated the city's populace.

tive, and judicial power. Instead, fragments of these powers were parceled out into various offices. The judicial power, for example, was shared among certain of the assemblies and the praetors. The executive power was divided among the consuls, praetors, senators, quaestors, and others. The legislative power, meanwhile, appertained to the various assemblies and to the Senate.

Like the ancient Greek city-states, Rome provided for deliberation and even the enactment of laws by the masses in popular assemblies. This serious flaw — the absence of representative government — guaranteed all of the instability and tumult associated with direct democracy, finally leading to the rise of unscrupulous demagogues.

Overall, the Roman Republic, even in its best years, was a far cry from the standards of liberty and peace to which modern Americans are accustomed. Rome was at war nearly all the time, and all able-bodied men were candidates for military service throughout their prime adult years. Roman citizens were bound by rigid class distinctions, and slavery was pervasive. Citizenship was generally not granted to subject peoples, even in Italy, until the first century B.C.

Above all else, it must be borne in mind that Rome was a pre-Christian civilization. Absent from Roman culture was the value on human life and individual dignity that has characterized enlightened states in Western Christian civilization. The Twelve Tables of Roman law required the killing of deformed infants, for example. Moreover, while the Roman military, at least during the republican period, acted with more restraint than was characteristic of the ancient world, their wars, battles, and sieges were nonetheless usually fought without negotiation and without quarter for the vanquished.

Legacy of Rome

The fall of Rome, although a tragedy to the generations that experienced it, has proven to be a blessing for mankind in the longer term. For while Rome's collapse led to a dark age of several centuries, it also made possible, in the longer run, the rise

Modern parallels: As the design of the U.S. Supreme Court alongside the Roman Pantheon attests, Roman architecture has had a profound influence on modern architectural styles. Rome lives on in her literature, language, law, art, and republican ideals.

of a modern civilization that has far eclipsed Rome's greatest achievements. Had Rome maintained indefinitely her grip on England, Anglo-Saxon civilization with its distinctive common law system could never have arisen. Germany would never have become civilized without the demise of the Roman legions that fought unceasingly to subdue her. The Italian city-state republics would never have inaugurated the Renaissance under the heel of the Roman military. Modern Western civilization, especially American civilization, with all of its blessings of freedom and progress, could never have been born under the banners of the Roman legions.

But Rome lives on in the fragments of Roman civilization that have inspired and guided her modern inheritors. It was a reawakening of interest in classical language and culture, particularly art and architecture, that motivated the pioneers of the Renaissance. Roman laws were the source of the civil law code of continental Europe, and had significant influence on English law as well. The Latin language has enriched modern English immeasurably, providing us with a vast scientific, academic, and legal lexicon.

Perhaps most importantly, America's Founding Fathers looked to Rome as their primary inspiration in learning the lessons of civilizations past, lessons extracted from striking historical parallels that modern Americans would do well to heed. Like America, Rome began as a tiny colony of immigrants surrounded by hostile neighbors. Like America, Rome was governed first by kings, and founded a republic when its monarchy turned into despotism. Like America, early Rome placed great importance on separating and limiting the powers of government. Like modern America, republican Rome embarked on a destructive program of foreign military adventurism that added to her international prestige but sapped her strength and resources. Like America, Rome succumbed to the temptations of the welfare state, teaching her citizens to divide into factions to fight over the spoils of the public treasury and to depend on government for their material well-being. Like America, Rome saw the rise of subversive movements that attacked her free constitution. And like the America in which we now live, Rome underwent a dizzying cultural and moral decline, which, in the case of Rome, eventually destroyed Rome's capacity for self-government.

In spite of the many parallels, there are also differences that suggest that America need not suffer the same fate as Rome. For one thing, in spite of the venality of modern American society, we are nowhere near the pitch of moral decline depicted in the pages of Suetonius, Tacitus, and Juvenal. For another, our Constitution is vastly superior to Rome's, and ought to prove far more durable. Most crucially, modern America possesses many layers of strength — cultural, moral, religious, institutional, and even technological — that ancient Rome did not have, that may allow America to endure where Rome faltered.

With all her tarnished greatness, Rome is a witness, not only of the pitfalls of power, prestige, and prosperity, but of the transcending truth that, even under the most adverse circumstances, freedom and enduring civilization are possible.

FOR FURTHER READING

The original sources for Rome's semi-legendary early history are many, but two in particular stand out, as much for their literary quality as for their historical interest: Livy and Plutarch. Titus Livius or Livy was, if not the greatest, certainly the most comprehensive source for Roman history, from the founding of Rome up to the late republican period. As with most ancient authors, much of Livy's Roman history has been lost, but the remaining portions are packed with fascinating details and vivid descriptions of pivotal events like the expulsion of the Tarquins. In the American Founders' day, Livy was required reading for advanced Latin students. Nowadays, the complete surviving works of Livy are available in very readable translation, and are one of the best introductions to both the history and culture of early Rome.

Plutarch, a Greek who compiled his famous book of parallel biographies of ancient Greeks and Romans in the early second century A.D., is one of the best-loved writers of all time. His brief but engaging sketches portray his subjects with honesty and affection; their failings and strengths are both held up for the reader to evaluate. Still the best translation of Plutarch's *Lives* — one of the most widely read books in early America — is the so-called Dryden translation. Compiled by poet John Dryden in the late 1600s and later edited by scholar Arthur Clough in the mid-19th century, this masterly translation is still in print in a two-volume Modern Library Classics edition.

Sources for the late Roman Republic are fairly detailed. Most of the best Roman historians lived in the early empire, and for them, the age of the Gracchi and the civil wars was fairly recent history. It was also the time of Rome's greatest pathos, of heroes and villains, of epic battles and world-convulsing political turmoil.

The best comprehensive source for the period extending from the Gracchi to the death of Sulla is undoubtedly Appian. For the events between 133 and 70 B.C., his is the only surviving continuous source. Like many of Rome's best historians, Appian was Greek. He was a native of Alexandria, born in the late first century A.D., and probably composed his history between 145 and 165 A.D., at the zenith of the Roman Empire under the Antonines. Living during a comparatively peaceful interlude, Appian, more than any other Roman historian, wrote with passion and dismay of the horrors of civil war and despotism. He deplored the destruction of the republic and traced many significant details — the conspiracies, the political rivalries, the assassinations, and the brutal personages — with unforgiving attention to detail that make his history the best all-around work for those wishing to understand the fall of the republic from an original source.

Besides chronicling Rome's civil wars, Appian also wrote volumes on Rome's many wars of conquest. His accounts of the Iberian, African, and Mithridatic wars are noteworthy for the author's sympathy with subjugated peoples and his unstinting criticism of Roman brutality. Appian's history of the civil wars is available in a fine Penguin paperback translation. The balance of his Roman history is available only in Loeb Classic hardcover editions, unlikely to be on the shelf at most local bookstores, but well worth the time and expense to order from the publisher.

Plutarch has given fine biographies of several of the personalities that figure in this book, including Sulla, Marius, and the Gracchi. Plutarch's character portraits, as always, seek to give balanced accounts, highlighting wherever possible the heroism as well as the villainy of his subjects.

A very readable source on the Jugurthine War is Sallust, a Roman politician who was a contemporary and friend of Julius Caesar. Many of Sallust's writings have been lost, but his two surviving complete works — a description of the Jugurthine War and an account of the Catilinarian conspiracy — are gems of conciseness, if not altogether historically accurate and sometimes encumbered by the author's undisguised biases. Both of Sallust's works are available in a single Penguin paperback translation.

Direct documentation of the Roman Empire and its decline is surprisingly sparse. The best sources for the first century A.D., Tacitus and Suetonius; both make grim if informative reading. Tacitus, lauded by many as the best Roman historian for his concision, attention to detail, and reliability, is a must-read for anyone wanting a dispassionate account of Roman culture and politics at the beginning of the Christian era. The surviving portions of Tacitus' two magisterial works on Roman history, *The Annals* and *The Histories*, are available complete in a Modern Library Classics paperback edition.

Tacitus' scandalous counterpart, Suetonius, is not for all tastes. Where Tacitus draws a curtain of discretion over the baser acts of his subjects, Suetonius unstintingly describes perversities that would make even some modern pornographers squirm with unease. The reader of Suetonius' *The Twelve Caesars*, available complete in a Penguin Paperbacks edition, must be prepared for an utterly candid view of diabolical levels of personal corruption. If nothing else, Suetonius is the most devastating testimony ever written of the dangers inherent in unlimited government power.

The last true Roman historian was Ammianus Marcellinus, who chronicled the events of his lifetime, many of which he witnessed. A professional soldier, he participated in Julian's disastrous Persian campaign. He lived to see the virtual destruction of the Roman Empire, and his history concludes with a vivid description of the Battle of Hadrianople. The Penguin Paperbacks edition of his history is nearly complete, but a few passages have been removed for editorial reasons.

Finally, no discussion of Roman sources would be complete without reference to the venerable Edward Gibbon, whose massive *History of the Decline and Fall of the Roman Empire* remains, more than two centuries after its original publication, the most comprehensive such history, and perhaps the greatest historical treatise on any subject ever written. That said, the authority of Gibbon is often overdrawn. His obvious command of the facts and copious documentation are often overshadowed by his pompous tone, overuse of certain stock words and phrases, and blatant hostility to Christianity. All writers are entitled to their prejudices, of course, but Gibbon attributes the fall of the Roman Empire largely to the rise of Christianity. There is ample reason to suppose instead that Christianity artificially prolonged the life of an otherwise moribund state. It was certainly the case that Byzantium, the heir of the Eastern Empire, lacked any semblance of good government, and was preserved mostly by the vitality of her faith.

Nor was Gibbon any great champion of republican virtue and liberty. He, like many elites of his age, was awed by empire and cared little for the bucolic virtues of early Rome. As a consequence Gibbon, despite the canonical status he now enjoys, was very controversial both in America and in Europe when his work was first published. Many early Americans preferred the now-forgotten world history of the Frenchman Abbé Millot, a less monumental work but infinitely friendlier to republican values than Gibbon. In sum, Gibbon is without parallel as a source of raw information, but less reliable as an interpreter of the events he chronicled.

INDEX

A

academic 118
Actium 92, 94, 100
Adriatic 1, 26
adulterers 60
adultery 102
Aegean 49, 70
Aeneas 1, 2
Aeneid, The 1
Aequans 3, 7, 21, 25
Africa 28, 29, 36, 50, 53, 54, 78, 80, 113
African 122
Africanus (see Scipio)
agrarian law 41
Agrippa 93, 95
Agrippa (the son) 100
Agrippina (mother of Nero) 103
Alan 98
Alans 98
Alaric 97, 99
Alba 6
Alba Longa 2
Albania 25
Albans 6
"Alea jacta est" ("The die is cast") 77
Alexandria 108, 122
Allobroges 63
Allucius 21, 22
Alps 23-24, 27, 46
America 124
American civilization 118
American Founders 121
Americans 116

America's Founding Fathers 118
Ammianus 99
Amulius 2
Anglo-Saxon civilization 118
Annals, The (by Tacitus) 123
Antiochus 30, 32
Antonines 122
Antoninus 106
Antonius, Caius 66
Antonius, Marcus (Mark Antony) 79-80, 85-88, 90-94, 114
Appian 1, 42, 50, 52-54, 64, 81, 112, 121, 122
Appian Way 47, 48
Appius 19
Appolonius 58
Aquae Sextiae (Aix-en-Provence) 46
Arausio 46
Archimedes 27
architecture 118
Arian Christian 109
Armenia 74
armies 23
Arpinium 62
art 118
Asculum 26
Asia Minor vii, 48, 49, 50, 70, 71, 72, 80, 90, 113
Asian 50, 55
Asiatic 109
assassination(s) 62, 78, 81, 82, 85, 102, 112, 114, 122
assassins 82-83, 85-87, 103
assemblies 43, 86, 116
Athenian Areopagus 4

Athens 10
Atilius, Marcus 6
Attila 97, 99
Augustan period 103
Aurelian 113
Aurelius, Marcus 106
austere virtues 33

B

Babylon vii
Babylonia 112
Bacchic 33
Bacchus 33
Balearic Islands 23
barbarian(s) 37, 98, 99, 108, 113
Battle of Hadrianople 123
Battle of Munda 80
Battle of Teutoburg Forest 3
Bithynia 71
blackmail 112
Bononia 88
bread and circuses 19
Brennus 20
bribery 112
Britain 74, 75
British 75
Brutus, Marcus Junius 55, 71, 81,
        85, 86, 88, 90, 91, 96, 111
Brutus, Lucius Junius 8, 9, 10
Byzantine Empire 111
Byzantium 22, 104, 113, 124

C

Caesar, Caius Julius 52, 55, 57-
        58, 64, 66-67, 69-74, 75-
        83, 85, 87-88, 90, 93-94,
        100, 113-114, 122
Caesar, Lucius 88
Caesar, Ptolemy (Caesarion) 93
Caesarian dictatorship 81

Caesarism 43, 67, 69, 82
Caesars 15, 111
Caesar Augustus (Octavian) 3, 6,
        95, 96, 101
Caius, Marius 45
Caligula 101, 106
Caligula (Gaius Germanicus) 102
Calpurnia (Caesar's wife) 81
Camillus, Marcus Furius 19, 20,
        21, 22, 32
Cannae 4, 23, 25, 27, 46, 99
Cantacuzenus, John 22
Capitol 21
Capitoline Hill 40
Capua 47
Caracalla 108
Carbo 53
Carrhae 3, 77, 113
Cartagena 21
Carthage vii, 3, 23, 26, 27, 28,
        31, 34-36, 37, 41, 43,
        44-45
Carthaginian 3, 24, 29
Carthaginians 25, 28, 34, 36, 112
"Carthago delenda est" ("Car-
        thage must be destroyed")
        34
Cassius 85, 86, 88, 90, 91
Cassius, Spurius 15
Catilinarian conspiracy 59, 61,
        122
Catilinarians 64
Catiline, Lucius 57, 58, 60, 61,
        62, 63, 64, 66, 112
Cato 55, 65, 66, 71, 74, 77
Cato the Elder 34
Cato the Younger (Cato, Marcus)
        64, 78, 80, 91
Caudine Forks 3
Celtic Britain 98

Cethegus 62, 63, 65
charisma 103
chastity 18, 19
checks and balances 114
Christ 71, 109
Christian 113
Christian civilization 112
Christian era 123
Christianity vii, 19, 104, 106, 108, 113, 124
Christians 103-105, 108
Cicero, Marcus Tullius 55, 57-64, 66, 71, 72, 74, 85-86, 88, 96, 111-112
Cilician pirates 58, 62, 70, 113
Cimbri 46
Cimbrian War 46
Cinna 50, 53, 71
Cinnilla, Cornelia 71
Citizenship 116
city-state 1
civil law code 118
civil unrest 39, 114
civil war(s) 43, 47, 48, 52, 54-55, 77, 90, 93, 106, 121, 122
civilized rule 103
class distinctions 116
class warfare 41
classical language 118
Claudius 102
Claudius, Appius 16-18, 42
Cleopatra 80, 92, 93-94
Clough, Arthur 121
Code of Hammurabi 17
code of laws vii, 4
Collatinus 9
Commodus 106, 108, 113
confederates 62
conspiracies 122
conspiracy 57, 59, 61, 63, 64, 66

conspirators 64, 65
Constantine the Great 106, 108
Constantinople 109
constitution 119
consul 80
consuls 53, 116
continental Europe 118
Corinth 30
Coriolanus 41
Crassus 3, 47-48, 55, 60, 66, 71, 74, 75
Crassus, Licinius 58
criminals 60
crucifixes 47
Ctesiphon 108
cultural 119
cultural and moral decline 119
culture (classical) 118
cut-throats 60

D

Dalmatia 108
Danube 97, 98
dark age 116
Dark Ages 108
death blow (of the republic) 82
Debauchees 60
debt 14
Decemvir(s) 15-19
decline and fall of republics 109
deliberation 116
demagogue(s) 39, 50, 71, 116
demagoguery 55
democracy(ies) 81, 93
Demosthenes 86
depravity 103
despotism 45, 50, 52, 55, 67, 109, 118, 122
dictator for life 80
dictators 114

Dio, Cassius 93, 95, 112
Diocletian 106, 108, 113
direct democracy 116
domestic liberties 114
domestic turmoil 96
Drusus 48
Dryden, John 121
Dyrrachium 76, 78

E

earthquake 108
Eastern Empire 109, 124
Ebro River 27
economic decay 99
Egypt vii, 78, 80, 92, 108
Egyptian 78
Elagabalus 108
Elam vii
elephants 23
emperor-worship 112
empire 85, 92, 95, 97, 98
enactment of laws 116
enduring civilization 119
England 118
English law 118
English Magna Charta 17
Epirus 3, 25
Eternal City 11, 13, 27
Etruscan 2, 14, 25
eulogy of Caesar 86
Europe vii, 124
"Even you, my child?" ("Et tu, Brutus?") 82
executive 114, 116
expansionism 109

F

Fabius Maximus 28
factions 118
Falerii 20

Faliscans 20
fall of Rome 116
Federalist Papers, The 10
Fetials 5
fire-raising 62
First Mithridatic War 50
First Plebeian Secession 14, 41
First Punic War 25, 26, 27
First Triumvirate 74, 77
flattery 71
foreign adventures 106
foreign military adventurism 118
Forum (Roman) 9, 10, 13, 14, 17, 18, 43, 82, 86, 111
Founding Fathers, America's vii, 10, 100
France 75
free constitution 118
free states 93
freedom 22, 93, 118, 119
Fritigern 98
Fulvia (Mark Antony's wife) 92
Fulvius, Quintus 29
Furies 40

G

Galba, Servus Sulpicius 32, 104
Gallic 21, 61, 75
Gallic Wars (Caesar's) 75
gamblers 60
Gaul 23, 46, 75, 99
Gauls 3, 11, 20, 25, 73, 77, 113
Geloni 97
Genseric 97, 107
German 46
Germania 81
Germanic 97, 107, 109
Germanicus 100-101
Germanicus, Gaius (Caligula) 101-102

Germans 3, 46, 113
Germany 118
Gerousia 4
Gibbon, Edward 106, 109
Gothic 113
Gothic horde 99
Goths 97, 98, 99, 109
Gracchi 15, 40-41, 50, 114, 121, 122
Gracchus, Caius 39, 41, 42, 43
Gracchus, Tiberius 39, 41, 42, 43
great conflagration 103, 105
Greece 15, 25, 30, 32, 58, 78, 88, 90, 99, 108
Greek 26, 50, 58, 109, 122
Greek city-states 30, 116
Greek legal code 15
Greeks 112, 121
Gulf of Actium 93

H

Hadrian 98, 106
Hadrian's Wall 98
Hadrianople 98, 99, 108
Hamilton, Alexander 3, 10
Hannibal Barca (Hannibal) 3, 4, 23, 24, 25, 27, 28, 29, 30, 32
heavy taxation 106
Hellenic world 30
Heraclea 26
Herod 100
Histories, The (by Tacitus) 123
History of the Decline and Fall of the Roman Empire, Edward Gibbon 106, 123
Hitler, Adolf 103
homosexual 102, 112
homosexuality 71
Hostilius, Tullus 6

human life 116
Hun(s) 97, 98, 99

I

Iberia 27, 28, 32, 43, 46, 113
Iberian 122
Iberian peninsula 23
Icilius 18
Ides of March, the 82, 91
Illyricum 25
immigrants 98, 118
immigration 98
imperial dominance 82
imperial expansion 25
Imperial Republic 23, 37
Imperial Rome 96, 106, 108, 111, 113
imperialism 96
individual dignity 116
informers 100
institutional 119
integrity 22
international warfare 114
Israel (ancient) 17
Istanbul 22
Italian 48, 50
Italian city-state republics 118
Italian peninsula 25
Italians 48
Italy 1, 23, 26, 27, 28, 29, 30, 54, 57, 62, 95, 96, 99, 116

J

Jay, John 10
Jerusalem 74, 104
Jews 104
judicial 116
Jugurtha 44-45
Jugurthine War 43, 49, 122
Julia (Caesar's daughter) 74, 75

Julian 113, 123
Julian ("the Apostate") 106, 108
Julius (July) 81
Jupiter 8
Juvenal 19, 119

K

kings 118

L

Lake Trasimene 23
Latin 25, 58, 111, 118, 121
Latins 2
Latinus 2
layers of strength 119
legal 118
legislative 114, 116
Lenas, Marcus Pompilius 32
Lentulus, Publius 62, 63, 64, 65
Lepanto 93
Lepidus 86, 88, 90, 92
liberty 4, 17, 55, 82, 86, 112, 116
Lives (by Plutarch) 121
Livius, Titus (Livy) 121
Livy 1, 2, 6, 7, 17, 28, 30, 121
Longinus, Gaius Cassius 81
Low Countries 75
Lucilius 91
Lucretia 8, 9
Lucullus 72
Lusitanian War 32
Lusitanians 32
luxury 33

M

Maccari 57
Macedonia 3, 32, 90
Macedonian 30
Madison, James 10

Maecenas 95
Magistrates 81, 112
Magna Graeca (Greater Greece) 26
Mamertines 26
Manlius, Titus 6
Marcellinus, Ammianus 98, 123
Marcellus, Marcus Claudius 28
Marcus (son of Cato the Younger) 91
Marius, Caius 3, 44, 46, 48, 49, 50, 53, 55, 71, 72, 77, 114, 122
Marius (the son) 53
martial virtues 113
martyrdom 105
massacre 62
masses 116
Massinissa 34, 44
mass executions 102
Maximin 108
Mediterranean 27, 30, 32, 34-36, 57, 70, 108
Melanchlaenae 97
Mesopotamia 74
Messalina (wife of Claudius) 103
Messina 26
Metella, Cornelia 75
Metellus 53, 66
mid-Mediterranean 72
Middle East vii
Miletus 70
militarism 44, 55, 109
military 74
military coups 114
military dictators 114
military dictatorship 100
military junta 90
military machine 82
military science 113

military service 3, 116
Millot, Abbé 100, 124
Mithra 112
Mithraism 113
Mithridates 3, 48, 49, 50-51, 55,
    60, 62, 70, 72, 80
Mithridatic 122
mob rule, 39
modern civilization 118
modern English 118
Molo, Appolonius 58
monarchy 60, 79, 95, 118
moral 112, 119
moral decline 112, 119
moral depravity 22
moral rectitude 19
moral strength 19
moral turpitude 66
morals 33

N

Nabis 30
Nasica, Scipio 43
Nero 101, 103-106
Nerva 106
noblemen 54
North Africa vii, 30, 32, 43, 46,
    72
North African 24, 44
Numa (Pompilius) 5, 6
Numantia 43
Numidia (North Africa) 23, 34,
    44
Numidians 34
Numitor 2

O

Octavia (Octavian's half-sister)
    92

Octavian (Caesar Augustus) 85-
    86, 88, 90, 91, 92, 93, 95,
    100, 114
Octavius 42, 50
Ofella, Quintus Lucretius 54
old republic 90
open borders 98
Optimates 77
opulence 82
Orange, France 46
Otho 104

P

Palestine 62, 74
Parthia 74, 75, 81
Parthia/Persia 77
Parthians 3, 75, 77, 113
patrician(s) 14, 15, 41-43, 62,
    114
patrician aristocracy 114
patronage 71
Paulus 88
Paulus, Lucius Aemilius 25
peace 116
peace, luxury, and security 82
perjurers 60
persecutions 103
Persia 112
Persian 112, 113, 123
Persian Empire 108
Pertinax 106, 108
perversions 103
Pharnaces II 80
Pharsalus 76, 78
Philip of Macedon 86
Philippi 88, 90
Philippics 86
pillaging 98
Pistoria 66
plebeian(s) 14-15, 17-18, 41, 114

Plutarch 2, 4, 5, 10, 12, 20, 54, 78, 80, 82, 88, 90, 106, 121, 122
pogroms 71
police state 100, 102
political 112
political rivalries 122
political turmoil 106
politician 71
politician-generals 47
Polybius 4
Pompeius, Gnaeus (Pompey) 53, 55, 58, 60, 62, 66, 71-72, 74-78, 82
Pompilius, Numa 4, 7
Pontus 3, 48, 50, 62, 70, 80
Poplicola (Publius Valerius) 10, 11, 22
popular assemblies 116
pornographers 123
Postumius, Spurius 33
Praeneste 54
Praetorian guards 108
praetors 53, 116
pre-Christian civilization 116
priesthood 112
profligates 60
Ptolemy 78
public entertainment 103
public treasury 118
public works 81
Punic wars 31, 113
Pyrrhus (king of Epirus) 3, 25, 26

Q

quaestors 116
Quinctius, Titus 30
Quintus (Julius, July) 81

R

radical dualism 112
redistribution of wealth and land 81
reign of terror 103
religious 112, 119
Renaissance 118
representative government 116
republic 64-65, 71, 77, 80, 81, 85, 95, 96, 97, 109, 112, 118
republic to empire 35, 85
republican 60
republican army 90, 91
republican forces 92
republican government 4, 93, 95
republican liberty 124
republican patriots 66
republican Rome 99, 104, 112, 113
republican virtue 124
republicanism 96
restore the republic 81
revolution 62, 63
Rhodes 55, 57
riots 114
Roman calendar 81
Roman cavalry 25
Roman citizens 16, 116
Roman civilization 55, 118
Roman constitution 114
Roman culture 123
Roman Empire 89, 97, 98, 99, 100, 106, 122, 123
Roman Gaul 74
Roman history 121
Roman imperial decline 99
Roman law(s) 17, 118
Roman liberty(ies) 112, 114
Roman military 104, 116

Roman North Africa 99
Roman Pantheon 117
Roman people 95
Roman Republic 2, 4, 5, 9, 10, 11, 12, 13, 14, 15, 17, 19, 22, 37, 51, 55, 69, 85, 100, 111, 112, 116, 121
Roman senate 33, 40, 57
Roman soldiers 8-9
Roman territory 98
Romans 121
Romulus 4, 6, 109
Romulus and Remus 2
rostra (in senate) 88
Rubicon River 52, 77
ruling class 114

S

Sabine 4
Sabines 2, 6
sacking of Rome 11, 97, 99, 107
Sallust 58, 60, 64, 65, 66, 112, 122
Samnite(s) 3
Sanga, Quintus Fabius 63
Sassanids 113
scientific 118
Scipio, Publius Cornelius (Africanus) 21, 22, 28, 29
Scipio Aemilianus 36, 37
Scythia 81
Scythian 97
Second Punic War 21, 23, 27, 28, 30, 34, 44, 99
Second Triumvirate 88, 90
secret society 112
self-government 83, 119
semi-secret political alliance 74

Senate 4, 7, 28, 29, 43, 44, 50, 53, 60, 61, 62, 63, 64, 72, 74, 77, 80, 82, 86, 95, 96, 106, 108, 116
senators 3, 10, 17, 21, 43, 50, 53, 54, 65, 82, 96, 102
separate and limited powers of government 118
separation of powers 114
Sextus 8
sexual depravity 100
sexual perversion 112
Sicilian 27
Sicily 25, 26, 27, 72, 108
slavery 93, 116
slaves 41, 42
Social War 48, 49, 53, 63
Solon 10, 15
soothsayer 82
sovereign 95
Spain 23, 29, 54, 55, 72, 80
Sparta 3, 4, 30
Spartacan revolt 47, 55
Spartacus 3, 47-48, 58, 72
spoils 118
subversive movements 118
Suetonius 100, 102, 103, 104, 119, 123
Sulla, Lucius (Sulla) 44, 48, 49, 50, 52-55, 58, 71, 72, 77, 81, 95, 114, 121, 122
Sumer vii
Surena 75
Syracuse (Sicily) 26, 27, 28
Syria 30, 32, 74

T

Tacitus 104, 106, 112, 119, 123
Tarentines 26
Tarentum 26, 27

Tarquinius, Collatinus 9
Tarquinius, Lucius, Superbus
     (Tarquin the Proud) 7, 9
Tarquins 2, 3, 9, 11, 19, 121
Tarquin the Proud 8, 9, 14, 17
taxes 14
technological 119
temple of Janus 96
Tenth Legion 77
Teutoberg 113
Teutones 45-46
Theodoric 109
Third Punic War 46
Thrace 98, 99
Tiber 2, 41
Tiberius 42, 96, 100-101
Titus 104
torture 102
Totila 109
traitors 64
Trajan 106
Transalpine Gaul 63
treason 100
Trebia 23
tribunes 15
Triumvirate 75, 91, 92
triumvirs 88
Trojans 1, 2
Troy 1, 37
tsunamis 108
Tullia 7
Tullianum 65
Tullius, Servius 7
Tullus (Hostilius) 6, 7
Tuscany 66
Twelve Caesars, The (by Sueto-
     nius) 123
Twelve Tables of Roman law 15-
     17, 116
tyranny(ies) 93, 97, 99

tyrants 90

U

undefended borders 99
United States of America vii
uprising 72

V

Valens 98, 99, 108
Valerius, Publius (Poplicola) 8,
     9, 10
Vandals 99, 107
Varro 3
Veii 7, 20
Venetian Republic 111
Vercellae 46
Vercingetorix 77
Vespasian 104
Vesta 1, 5
vestal virgin(s) 1, 5, 103
vice(s) 60, 103
Virgil 1
Virginia 18, 19
Virginius 18, 19
Viriathus 32
Vitellius 104
Volscians 3, 7, 21, 25, 41

W

war 14
warfare 96, 99
welfare-warfare state 39
welfare state 118
welfarism 109
Western Christendom 111
Western Christian civilization
     116
Western civilization vii, 10, 82,
     113, 118

Western Roman Empire 109
written laws 15-16

Y

youth (corruption of) 60

Z

Zama 30

About the Author

Steve Bonta received his B.A. from Penn State University in 1989 in Comparative Literature, his M.A. in linguistics from Brigham Young University in 1996, and his PhD in the same subject from Cornell University in 2004. Dr. Bonta is proficient in several foreign languages, including Spanish and Sanskrit, and has traveled and lived across the globe in such places as South America, Asia, and Europe.

Dr. Bonta has written extensively for *The New American* magazine, the flagship publication of The John Birch Society, and is the author of the book *Inside the United Nations: A Critical Look at the UN*. Dr. Bonta teaches at Penn State University, and is the Communications Director for the Constitution Party. He and his family reside in Pennsylvania.

The Rise and Fall
OF THE
Roman Republic
Lessons for Modern America

To order additional copies of *The Rise and Fall of the Roman Republic*, call 1-800-342-6491, or visit American Opinion Book Services online at *www.aobs-store.com*.

And while you are online, check out the wide selection of additional education materials designed to build better citizens — and a better America.

The chapters in this book are adapted from a series of articles originally appearing in *The New American*, a biweekly magazine.

To subscribe, call 1-800-727-8783 or visit us at *www.thenewamerican.com*.